STORYTELLING IN PHARMA MARKETING

STORYTELLING IN PHARMA MARKETING

Subba Rao Chaganti

™ **PharmaMed Press**

An imprint of BSP Books Pvt. Ltd.
4-4-309/316, Giriraj Lane,
Sultan Bazar, Hyderabad - 500 001.

Storytelling in Pharma Marketing
by Subba Rao Chaganti

Published by:

™ **PharmaMed Press**
An imprint of BSP Books Pvt. Ltd.
4-4-309/316, Giriraj Lane, Sultan Bazar, Hyderabad - 500 001.
Phone: 040-23445688
E-mail: info@pharmamedpress.com
www.pharmamedpress.com/pharmamedpress.net

ISBN: 978-93-49562-03-5 (Hardback)

DISCLAIMER

This book is intended for informational and educational purposes only. The content presented herein reflects the author's research, knowledge, and professional insights into the role of storytelling in pharmaceutical marketing. While every effort has been made to ensure accuracy, completeness, and relevance, the information should not be considered professional, legal, regulatory, or medical advice.

Pharmaceutical marekting is a highly regulated field, and compliance with industry guidelines, ethical standards, and local regulatory requirements is essential. Readers are encouraged to consult relevant regulatory authorities, legal professionals, or compliance experts before applying any strategies or practices discussed in this book. The examples, case studies, and references included are for illustrative purposes only and do not imply endorsement of any specific company, product, or approach.

The author and publisher disclaim any liability for any direct or indirect consequences arising from using, interpreting, or applying the information provided in this book. The responsibility for ensuring adherence to applicable laws, regulations, and best practices remains with the reader.

All trademarks, brand names, and corporate references mentioned in this book are the property of their respective owners. Any resemblance to real-life situations or entities beyond cited case studies is purely coincidental.

By reading this book, the reader acknowledges and accepts this disclaimer.

-Author

ACKNOWLEDGMENTS

Writing a book is never a solitary journey. It is shaped by the encouragement, support, and contributions of many individuals, and I am deeply grateful to each one of them.

First and foremost, I sincerely thank my publishers, Anil Shah and Nikunjesh Shah, for their unwavering support and belief in this book. I especially thank Nikunjesh Shah for making the digital editions available and ensuring they reach a wider audience.

I also deeply appreciate Naresh Davergave and his talented team at PharmaMedPress for their dedication to designing this book with precision and professionalism. Their meticulous work has brought this book to life in a way that reflects the depth and significance of its content.

A special thanks to Srinivasa Phanindra for designing a beautiful cover for this book.

I want to express my heartfelt thanks to my family—my pillar of strength and inspiration. My beloved wife, Mahalakshmi, whose patience, love, and encouragement have been my greatest support throughout this journey. My children and their spouses—Srinivasa Phanindra, Geetha, Lavanya, Satya Shankara Aditya, Sowmya, and Chaitanya—for their belief in me and for always being my source of motivation.

A special mention to my wonderful grandchildren—Aditi, Eesha, Surya, and Shriya—Whose boundless curiosity and joy remind me of the importance of storytelling in shaping minds and inspiring generations.

To all my readers, colleagues, and well-wishers, thank you for your continued support and encouragement. Your interest in the evolving landscape of pharmaceutical marketing and storytelling fuels my passion for writing and sharing knowledge.

With deep appreciation

-Author

PREFACE

Storytelling has been an integral part of human communication for centuries. From ancient myths and legends to modern-day brand narratives, stories have shaped cultures, influenced decisions, and built lasting connections. Storytelling may seem like an unexpected tool in pharmaceutical marketing—a domain often seen as driven by data, regulations, and scientific rigor. Yet, it is precisely the power of narratives that enables brands to bridge the gap between complex science and human emotions, transforming mere information into meaningful engagement.

When I began my journey in pharmaceutical marketing, I noticed a common challenge: How do we make scientific information resonate with our audiences? How do we connect with physicians, patients, caregivers, and other stakeholders in a way that educates and inspires action? Traditional marketing approaches often fell short, overwhelmed by technical jargon or compliance constraints. The missing piece was storytelling—a strategic, evidence-based approach to communication that brings data to life, fosters trust, and creates lasting impact.

This book is my attempt to combine the science and art of storytelling, specifically tailored for the pharmaceutical industry. It is not about crafting engaging narratives; It is about understanding why stories work, how they shape perceptions, and what makes them effective in an industry bound by strict regulations and ethical considerations.

Throughout this book, you will explore:

- The psychology and neuroscience of storytelling — Why humans are wired for stories and how they influence decisions.
- The evolution of storytelling in marketing — How narratives have shaped brand success across industries, including pharma.
- The framework for effective storytelling — A step-by-step guide to crafting impactful, patient-centric, and brand-aligned narratives.

- Real-world case studies — Examples of successful storytelling strategies from within and outside pharma.
- The Role of AI, digital transformation, and emerging technologies — How storytelling evolves in the age of AI, AR/VR, and personalized marketing.

Whether you are a brand manager, marketing leader, medical affairs professional, sales executive, or communications strategist, this book will equip you with the tools and insights to create stories that resonate, educate, and inspire.

Pharmaceutical marketing is no longer just about selling a product—it is about making a difference in people's lives. And stories have the power to do just that.

Let's begin this journey together.

Subba Rao Chaganti
April 2025

CONTENTS

Part I. The Foundations of Storytelling

Before we explore the magic storytelling can create in pharma marketing, let's consider its foundations. Great storytelling isn't just about stringing words together; it's about tapping into something much deeper, something timeless.

At its heart, storytelling is how humans make sense of the world. Long before there were books, apps, or social media, people sat around fires, telling stories—about the hunt, the stars, the gods, the lessons learned. These stories weren't just entertainment, but also how knowledge, values, and emotions were passed from generation to generation.

The secret ingredient? Emotion?

Every memorable story touches some emotion—hope, fear, pride, love, loss, or triumph. Stories make facts feel real. They turn dry information into something people can connect with, remember, and act on. Even today, in our data-driven world, emotion moves people first, followed by logic.

Another core principle is structure?

Almost every great story follows a familiar rhythm:

- A character (someone relatable)
- Faces a challenge (conflict or problem)
- Overcomes it (resolution or transformation)

Think about it: whether it's a blockbuster movie, a bedtime fairy tale, or a patient's journey to recovery, this pattern keeps us engaged and rooting for the outcome.

And finally, authenticity is non-negotiable.

People are more skeptical than ever today. They can spot a polished, inauthentic story a mile away. The best stories come from real experiences, emotions, and human truths.

So, when we talk about storytelling in pharma marketing, it's not about spinning a tale. It's about revealing the truth in a way that resonates—showing the human side of healthcare, the hope behind the science, and the shared journey between patients, physicians, caregivers, and brands.

At its foundation, storytelling isn't a "nice to have" anymore. It's the oldest—and still the most powerful—way to make people care.

CHAPTER

1

Introduction to Storytelling

Let's start with a simple question: When was the last time you heard a story that stuck with you? Maybe it was a movie that moved you to tears, a childhood bedtime story that still makes you smile, or a personal anecdote from a friend that made you see the world differently.

Now, think about the last time you read a dry, data-heavy report. Do you remember anything from it? Probably not much.

That's the difference between information and storytelling. Facts inform, but stories transform.

Why Do We Love Stories?

Imagine sitting around a campfire thousands of years ago. The village elder tells a tale about heroes, gods, love, and loss. These stories were not just for entertainment; they were how wisdom, traditions, and survival tips were passed down.

Fast-forward to today, and we still do the same thing with different tools. Instead of a campfire, we have movies, books, social media, and, yes, even pharmaceutical marketing.

At its core, storytelling is how humans make sense of the world. It's why we remember powerful speeches, cry at movies, and connect with certain brands on a deeper level.

The Science Behind Storytelling

Here is where it gets fascinating: our brains are wired for stories.

- When we hear raw facts, only the language-processing part of our brain is engaged.
- When we hear a story, multiple areas light up —our sensory, emotional, and motor regions. If someone tells you about a delicious meal, your brain imagines the taste and smell. If they describe an exciting adventure, your brain feels the adrenaline.

This is why storytelling is such a powerful communication tool. It does not just tell people something — it makes them feel it.

Storytelling in Pharma Marketing: Why It Matters

Now, let's return to pharma marketing. Traditionally, the industry has relied on numbers, clinical trial results, and technical data. While those are important, they don't inspire action on their own.

Let's compare two ways of introducing a new diabetes treatment:

- **Approach 1 (Facts Only):**

  " This drug reduces A1C levels by 25% in clinical trials and has shown a 30% improvement in insulin sensitivity."
- **Approach 2 (Storytelling):**

  "Sarah, a 45-year-old mother of two, struggled with diabetes for years. No matter what she tried, she could not get her sugar levels under control. But when her doctor introduced her to this new treatment, everything changed. Now. Sarah has more energy to play with her kids and finally feels in control of her health again."

Which one is more engaging? The second one, of course! Why? Because it humanizes the data.

This is why storytelling is the future of pharmaceutical marketing. It builds trust, makes brands more relatable, and increases engagement with patients, healthcare professionals, and other stakeholders.

The Journey Ahead

In this book, we will explore:

- The science behind why stories work.
- How pharma can craft meaningful narratives.
- Real-world examples of storytelling in action.
- The role of AI, digital media, and new technologies in shaping storytelling.

By the end, you will see that storytelling is not just a nice-to-have in pharmaceutical marketing—it's an absolute necessity. Let's get started!

The Power of Stories

Think about the last time you got lost in a good story. Maybe it was a gripping novel, a binge-worthy TV show, or even a personal anecdote from a friend. Whatever it was, for a moment, you were not just listening — you were experiencing it.

That is the magic of storytelling. It does not just capture attention; it captures emotion. And emotion drives action.

Stories Stick, Facts Fade

Here is a little test.

Try to remember a commercial you saw last week that was packed with statistics. Hard, right? Now, think about the last ad that told a compelling story — maybe it was about an athlete overcoming adversity, a heartwarming moment between a father and daughter, or even a patient finding hope. That one? You probably remember.

Why? Because our brains are wired to remember stories, not just information. Research shows that people remember stories 22 times more than facts alone.

That is a game-changer for marketing, especially in an industry like pharma, where complex data often takes center stage.

Why Do Stories Work So Well?

Stories work because they engage multiple parts of our brain:

- **Logic + Emotion**: While facts activate only the analytical part of the brain, stories engage the emotional centers, making the information more memorable.
- **Empathy in Action**: When we hear a story, we don't just understand it—we feel it. Whether the story is about pain, triumph, or hope, our brain releases oxytocin, the same chemical linked to trust and human connection.

- **Mental Movies**: Stories help people visualize concepts. Instead of just hearing about a drug's efficacy, they can see how it changes someone's life.

The Power of Stories in Pharma Marketing

In pharma marketing, trust is everything. And nothing builds trust like an authentic, relatable story. For example, compare these two messages:

- **Traditional Approach:**

  "Our medication is clinically proven to reduce migraine frequency by 60%."
- **Storytelling Approach:**

  " For years, Emily dreaded waking up, unsure if a migraine would ruin her day. She missed family events, struggled at work, and felt helpless. But after starting this treatment, she has regained control of her life — attending her daughter's recital, enjoying weekends, and waking up without fear."

Which one feels more impactful? Which one makes you care? That is the power of storytelling. It transforms a statistic into a human experience.

Stories Move People to Act

Great stories do not just inform; they inspire action. Whether it's a patient asking their doctor about a treatment, a physician considering a new therapy, or even an internal team feeling more connected to their brand, stories drive behavior.

This is why pharma marketers who master storytelling stand out. In a sea of data and regulations, brands that connect on a human level will truly make an impact.

One thing is clear: if you want people to listen, remember, and care — tell them a story.

Why Stories Resonate with Humans

Have you ever heard a story that gave you chills? Maybe a movie that made you cry, a speech that inspired you, or even a simple childhood tale that still lingers in your mind?

That's because stories don't just pass through our ears — they sink into our hearts and minds.

We are Wired for Stories

From the moment we are born, we crave stories. As kids, bedtime stories were more than just entertainment — they helped us understand the world, process emotions, and make sense of right and wrong. Even as adults, we constantly seek narratives, whether in books, social media, or how we recall our daily experiences. And guess what? Science backs this up.

- Stories engage multiple areas of the brain. While facts light up only the language-processing center, stories activate regions linked with emotions, memory, and even motor responses. This is why when someone tells us about a delicious meal, we almost taste it. Or when we hear about a scary situation, our heart races.
- Stories trigger oxytocin, the "trust hormone." This chemical makes us feel empathy, connection, and even generosity. It is why we feel deeply for fictional characters or are moved by a stranger's inspiring journey.
- We think in stories, not in data. If I give you a list of numbers, you will forget them in minutes. But if I tell you a powerful story tied to those numbers, you will remember it for years.

Stories Make Us Feel, and Feelings Drive Decisions

Let's say you are choosing between two medications:

1. One is backed by a ton of clinical data but presented in a cold, fact-heavy format.

2. The other has data, too, but also shares a story about a patient who regained their life because of it.

Which one would stick with you more? Which one would make you care?

In pharmaceutical marketing, trust is everything. Trust is not built by numbers alone—it is built by human connection.

The Mirror Effect: Why We See Ourselves in Stories

One of the most powerful ways we connect with stories is through mirroring. When we hear a compelling story, our brains do not process the information—we live it.

- We see ourselves as the protagonist. Their struggles feel like our struggles. Their victories feel like our victories.
- We anticipate what happens next. This keeps us engaged. Our brains crave resolution, which is why we stay glued to a good story.
- We internalize lessons without even realizing it. Have you ever learned a moral from a fable? Stories teach without lecturing, making complex concepts digestible and relatable.

Why This Matters for Pharma Marketing

Pharma is an industry built on science, but at its core, it's about people. Patients. Doctors. Caregivers.

If you want people to:

- Trust a brand
- Feel connected to a treatment
- Take action

...then you need to tell a story that resonates with them.

So, the next time you want to share information — whether with patients, healthcare professionals, or even your internal teams — ask yourself:

- Is this just a fact, or is it a story?
- Does it make people feel something?
- Can they see themselves in it?

Because when people connect, they remember. And when they remember, they act.

That's why storytelling is not just powerful — it is essential.

The Role of Storytelling in Communication

Imagine sitting in a meeting where someone is presenting a new marketing strategy. One person delivers a dry PowerPoint filled with bullet points and numbers, while another shares a compelling story about how a similar strategy transformed a struggling brand into a market leader.

Who do you think will capture the audience's attention? More importantly, whose message will be remembered?

That's the power of storytelling in communication.

Why Storytelling Works for Communication

Communication is not just about transmitting information — it's about ensuring it is understood, remembered, and acted upon. And stories do this far better than plain facts. Here is why:

- **Stories Make Complex Information Simple**

  Ever struggled to explain a technical concept? Instead of listing facts, turn them into a story.

  That's why doctors use metaphors to explain diseases and why financial experts compare saving money to planting trees. Stories take abstract or complex ideas and make them relatable and digestible.

- **Stories Create Emotional Connections**

  People may forget what you said, but they will remember how you made them feel. A story taps into emotions, making communication more engaging and persuasive.

- **Stories Enhance Retention**

  Studies show that people remember up to 22 times more when information is presented in a story rather than a list of facts. This is crucial in pharmaceutical marketing, where messages need to stick —whether it is a doctor recalling a treatment's benefits or a patient remembering why adherence matters.

The Role of Storytelling in Different Types of Communication

1. **Marketing and Branding**: Great brands don't just sell products; they tell stories. Whether Nike's stories of perseverance or a pharma brand highlighting a patient's journey, stories make brands relatable and memorable.
2. **Healthcare & Pharma Communication**: Doctors and patients are bombarded with scientific jargon. But a well-crafted patient story can bring data to life, making it more compelling than a list of trial results.
3. **Leadership & Corporate Communication**: Want to inspire employees? Leaders who communicate through storytelling are more trusted and impactful. Instead of saying, "We need to be more innovative," a leader who shares a real-life success story about an employee's groundbreaking idea makes the message more powerful.
4. **Sales & Training**: Sales reps who share success stories instead of product specs are more persuasive. Training programs that use storytelling help employees retain and apply information better.

Bringing it all Together

Storytelling is not just a nice-to-have — It's a must-have in effective communication. Whether you are marketing a brand, educating patients, or motivating a team, the key to getting your message across and making it stick lies in the story you tell.

So, next time you communicate, ask yourself:

- Am I just giving information, or am I telling a story?
- Will my audience feel something?
- Will they remember this?

Because in the end, the best communicators are not just speakers — they are storytellers!

CHAPTER

2

The Science of Storytelling: Why Our Brains Crave Stories

Ever wonder why you can binge-watch an entire TV series in one weekend but struggle to remember a list of facts from a textbook? Or why does a powerful TED talk stick with you while a dry PowerPoint presentation fades from memory?

It is not magic — it is science. Our brains are literally wired for stories.

Your Brain on Stories: A Chemical Reaction

When we hear a story, something amazing happens in our brains. Unlike plain facts, which activate just the language-processing centers, stories light up multiple regions — including those responsible for emotions, sensory experiences, and motor functions.

Dopamine: The Focus Booster

Have you ever been hooked on a great book or a gripping movie? That is dopamine at work. This neurotransmitter increases when we hear a compelling story, keeping us engaged and helping us retain information longer.

Oxytocin: The Trust Builder

Oxytocin, often called the "trust hormone," is released when we hear an emotional story. It strengthens empathy and connection, which is why we root for underdogs in movies and why patient stories in pharma marketing are so powerful.

Mirror Neurons: The "Living the Story" Effect

Have you ever flinched during an action scene in a movie? Or did you feel sad when a character lost someone? That is because of mirror neurons — brain cells that make us feel like we are experiencing what we see or hear. This is why stories don't just inform us; they move us.

How Stories Shape Our Thinking and Decisions

1. **Stories Activate More of the Brain Than Facts Alone**

   If I tell you, "This drug reduced blood sugar levels by 20% in clinical trials, "your brain processes it as raw data. But if I say, "After struggling with diabetes for years, Sarah Finally found relief with this treatment, regaining the energy to play with her grandkids," Your brain visualizes Sarah's joy, feels her relief, and remembers the message better.

2. **Emotions Drive Decisions, Not Just Logic**

   We like to think we make decisions logically, but research shows that emotions play a dominant role. Stories influence how we feel about brands, products, and even medical treatments, because we are more likely to take action when we feel something.

3. **Stories Help Us Make Sense of the World**

   Humans crave struture. Stories provide a beginning, middle, and end, helping us make sense of complex topics. This is why pharma marketers should use storytelling to explain treatments, educate patients, and connect with doctors in a natural and compelling way.

The Takeaway: Use Science to Tell Better Stories

If you want your audience to remember, trust, and act on your message, don't just give them facts—tell them a story that taps into their emotions, activates their brains, and makes them feel personally connected.

Because at the end of the day, we don't just process stories —we live them. And that makes all the difference.

The Psychological and Neurological Basis of Stories: Why We Are Wired for Them

Have you ever found yourself completely absorbed in a movie, feeling the character's emotions as if they were your own? Or have you ever remembered a story from childhood with vivid detail while forgetting what you had for lunch yesterday?

That is not a coincidence. It's science.

Our Brains Crave Stories

Stories are not just entertainment — they are hardwired into our brains. Before we had books, science, or written language, we told stories. They helped us survive, pass down knowledge, and connect with others. That's why, even today, our brains react to stories differently than plain facts. Here is how:

1. **Stories Activate the Whole Brain (Not Just Language Centers)**

   When we hear a list of facts, only the language-processing part of the brain lights up. But when we hear a story, multiple brain regions come alive:

   - The sensory cortex engages if the story describes taste, smell, or touch.
   - The motor cortex activates if the story involves movement.
   - The emotional centers light up when the story makes us feel something.

   In other words, stories don't just tell us something — they make us experience it.

2. **Dopamine: The Engagement and Memory Booster**

   Ever wonder why cliffhangers keep you hooked? That's dopamine at work. When a story has suspense, curiosity, or emotional highs and lows, our brain releases this "feel-good" chemical, which:

- Keeps us focused (we want to know what happens next)
- Strengthens memory (we retain emotionally charged information longer)
- Enhances learning (we absorb concepts more deeply when they are tied to stories)

That's why patients are more likely to remember a health message told through a personal story than raw statistics.

3. **Oxytocin: The Trust and Connection Hormone**

   Why do we feel connected to people in stories, even fictional characters? The answer is oxytocin, the "trust hormone." When we hear a story that evokes empathy, our brain releases oxytocin, which:

   - Increases trust and emotional bonding
   - Makes us care about the characters or the message
   - Influences decision-making in favor of the storyteller

   This is why patient stories are so powerful for pharmaceutical marketers. A well-told story about a patient's journey can make doctors and stakeholders emotionally invest in treatment far more than a clinical trial graph ever could.

4. **Mirror Neurons: The "Living the Story" Effect**

   Ever watched a movie where someone got hit, and you physically flinched? That's because of mirror neurons — specialized brain cells that make us feel like we are experiencing what we see or hear. When we hear an engaging story:

   - Our brain mirrors the emotions of the storyteller or character.
   - We feel the joy, pain, or excitement as if it's happening to us.
   - This creates a stronger emotional connection, making the message stick.

   That is why storytelling in pharmaceutical is not just about informing — it's about immersing the audience in a narrative they emotionally connect with.

The Big Takeaway — Use Storytelling to Trigger the Right Brain Responses

If you want your audience — whether they are doctors, patients, or other stakeholders —to remember, trust, and act on your message, use storytelling to:

- Engage multiple parts of the brain for better retention
- Trigger dopamine to sustain attention and increase learning
- Release oxytocin to build trust and emotional connection
- Activate mirror neurons to make the audience feel personally involved

Because, in the end, facts tell, but stories sell. And the science proves it.

Emotional Connection and Decision-Making

How Stories Shape Our Emotions and Decisions

Imagine you are watching a heartfelt video about a child whose life was saved by a new treatment. You see her laugh, play, and hug her parents. By the end, you feel deeply moved — and if asked to support the cause behind that treatment, you would likely say yes.

Now, contrast this with reading a research paper filled with statistics on the treatment's success rate. While the statistics may be impressive, they don't move you.

That's the power of emotional connection in decision-making.

Emotions Drive Decisions, Not Logic

We like to think we make rational decisions based on logic and facts. But in reality, our brains don't work that way. Research in neuroscience and behavioral psychology shows that emotions play the biggest role in decision-making.

- A famous study by neuroscientist Antonio Damasio found that people with damage to the emotional centers of their brains struggled to make even the simplest decisions, even though their logical reasoning centers were intact.
- Why? Because decisions are not just about weighing pros and cons. They are about feeling what is right.

This is why storytelling is so powerful in marketing, especially in the pharmaceutical industry, where choices often involve health, trust, and deeply personal stakes.

How Stories Create Emotional Connection

Stories connect with us because they trigger empathy — the ability to feel what another person is experiencing. This happens through mirror neurons (which make us “live” the story) and the release of oxytocin, the hormone that builds trust and emotional bonds.

- We root for characters. When we hear patients’ journeys, we emotionally invest in their struggles and triumphs.
- We feel the stakes. A well-told story makes us care about the outcome, making it more memorable.
- We make decisions based on emotion and then justify them with logic. That’s why a compelling pharma brand story can drive brand preference far more effectively than a clinical data sheet alone.

The Pharma Connection: Why This Matters in Healthcare Marketing

Think about a doctor choosing between two equally effective medications. One brand presents dry clinical data, while the other shares a real patient story alongside the science. Which one leaves a lasting impression?

Or consider a patient hesitant about taking a new therapy. Will a list of side effects and efficacy percentages persuade them, or will a story of someone like them who regained their quality of life be more convincing?

This is why pharma marketers need to master storytelling. It is not about ignoring science — it is about bringing science to life through human experiences.

The Takeaway: To Influence Decisions, Make People Feel

If you want your audience — whether doctors, patients, or other stakeholders — to take action:

- Trigger emotions first. Facts inform, but emotions persuade.

- Use patient and physician stories. Real experiences make data relatable.
- Make the audience see themselves in the story. Personal relevance strengthens impact.

Because, in the end, we don't buy into facts — we buy into feelings. And storytelling is the bridge that connects both.

CHAPTER

3

What is Storytelling in Pharma Marketing?

Imagine a doctor sitting through yet another scientific presentation filled with dense data, charts, and regulatory jargon. Now, imagine a different approach — where the speaker shares a real-life story about a patient whose life was transformed by a breakthrough therapy. The doctor leans in, listens closely, and remembers the message long after the presentation ends.

That is the power of storytelling in pharmaceutical marketing. It turns complex science into compelling narratives that resonate with patients, healthcare professionals (HCPs), and other stakeholders on an emotional level.

Defining Storytelling in Pharma Marketing

At its core, pharmaceutical storytelling is about using narrative techniques to communicate medical, scientific, and brand messages in a way that engages, educates, and inspires action. It is not about selling a product; it is about creating meaningful connections through stories that humanize science and medicine.

A good pharma story does not just say, "This drug improves lung function by 35%." It tells the story of a patient who once struggled to climb stairs but can now chase after their grandkids because of that treatment.

It is about moving from features and benefits to human impact.

Why is Storytelling Important in Pharma?

Unlike consumer brands, pharma operates in a highly regulated, evidence-based environment. But that does not mean storytelling is not essential—it is even more crucial.

Here is why:

- Science alone does not sell. Doctors and patients do not just want data; they want to know how a treatment changes lives.
- Healthcare decisions are emotional. Fear, hope, trust, and uncertainty play a big role in treatment decisions — stories tap into these emotions.
- It makes information memorable. Studies show that people remember stories 22 times more than facts alone.
- It builds trust. Patients and HCPs are bombarded with claims, and authentic storytelling makes brands more credible and relatable.

The Elements of Effective Storytelling in Pharma

A great pharma marketing story follows the classic storytelling structure:

- Hero — The patient, doctor, or caregiver facing a challenge.
- Conflict — The medical condition, treatment barrier, or emotional struggle.
- Resolution — How the treatment or solution changes their lives.

The best pharma stories:

- Put people at the center — Focus on patient experiences, physician perspectives, or real-world challenges.
- Are authentic — Avoid over-promising or dramatizing; real stories work best.
- Use data to support emotion — Stories backed by scientific credibility build trust.
- They are adapted to different audiences — Patients, doctors, and regulators need different storytelling approaches.

Where Does Storytelling Fit in Pharma Marketing?

Storytelling can be used across multiple touchpoints:

- Patient education materials – Turning medical jargon into relatable experiences.
- HCP engagement – Using real-world case studies to illustrate treatment impact.
- Brand campaigns – Building emotional connections with audiences.
- Corporate storytelling – Showcasing a company's mission, innovation, and values.

The Future of Storytelling in Pharma

With digital tools, AI, and immersive technologies like VR and AR, pharmaceutical storytelling is evolving. Companies are now using:

- Video stories – Real patient journeys in documentary-style formats.
- AI-driven personalization – Tailoring narratives to specific HCP or patient profiles.
- Virtual Reality Experiences – Letting HCPs "step into a patient's shoes."

The bottom line? Storytelling in pharmaceuticals is not a "nice-to-have"—it is a "must-have." It is how brands cut through the noise, build trust, and drive real-world impact.

Because, at the end of the day, people do not remember statistics – they remember stories.

Definition and Scope of Storytelling in Pharma Marketing

Let us start with a simple truth: facts tell, but stories sell — and nowhere is this more relevant than in pharmaceutical marketing.

Think about it. If you are a pharma brand manager, you are not just selling a drug; you are selling hope, relief, and a better quality of life. But how do you communicate that effectively? Through storytelling.

When we talk about storytelling in pharma marketing, we mean using narratives to make scientific and medical information engaging, memorable, and emotionally resonant.

It is not about making things up or embellishing reality — it is about framing facts in a way that connects with people on a deeper level. It is about humanizing science.

So, What is the Scope?

The scope of storytelling in pharma marketing is vast, touching every part of the industry—from patient education to doctor engagement and even corporate branding.

Here is where storytelling plays a role:

1. **Patient-Centric Storytelling: Making Science Relatable**

   Patients are not just looking for medical information — they want to see themselves in the stories they encounter.

   - **Before & After Journeys:** Patient experiences showing life before and after treatment.
   - **Empowerment Stories:** Stories that educate and inspire patients to take control of their health.
   - **Myth-Busting Stories:** Addressing misconceptions about diseases and treatments.

Example: A campaign for an insulin brand that follows the story of a teenager managing diabetes, showing how the treatment fits into their daily life.

2. **Physician Engagement: Moving Beyond Data-Heavy Marketing**

   Doctors are scientists at heart, but they are also human. Facts alone do not always persuade, but facts wrapped in a compelling story? That's a game-changer.

   - **Clinical Case Studies as Stories:** Instead of just sharing data, tell the story of a real patient case.
   - **Emotional Hooks in Medical Education:** Using narratives to highlight the urgency of diagnosing conditions early.
   - **Pharma Rep Training:** Teaching sales teams to communicate science through impactful storytelling.

   Example: A medical conference keynote that does not just show clinical trial results but tells the story of a physician who saw firsthand how a new cancer drug saved a patient.

3. **Corporate and Brand Storytelling: The 'Why' Behind Pharma Companies**

   People trust companies with a purpose. Pharma brands are not just about selling.

   - **Medications:** They are about solving healthcare challenges and improving lives.
   - **Brand Mission Stories:** Why the company was founded and what it stands for.
   - **Innovation Narratives:** Showcasing the journey of a drug from discovery to market.
   - **CSR & Patient Advocacy Stories:** Sharing how a company makes a difference beyond profits.

Example: A pharma company launching a rare disease drug shares the story of the researchers who worked for years to develop the treatment against all odds.

4. **Digital and AI-Powered Storytelling: The Future is Here**

   With digital transformation, storytelling is going beyond traditional ads and brochures.

   Now, brands are using:

   - **Video & Documentary-Style Stories:** Bringing real patient experiences to life.
   - **AI-Driven Personalization:** Customizing narratives based on patient profiles.
   - **Virtual & Augmented Reality:** Immersive storytelling experiences for HCPs and patients.

   Example: A VR experience that allows doctors to "see through the eyes" of a migraine patient, creating empathy and understanding of the condition.

Final Thoughts: Why Scope Matters

The scope of storytelling in pharmaceuticals is not just about selling a product. It is also about building trust, educating stakeholders, and making complex science seem human.

Pharma marketing does not have to be cold and technical — it can be inspiring, relatable, and emotionally engaging.

Because, at the end of the day, people don't connect with molecules — they connect with stories.

Unique Challenges in Pharma Marketing: Why Storytelling Isn't Always Easy

Pharma marketing is not like selling sneakers, coffee, or the latest smartphone. You are not just convincing people to buy something—you are often trying to educate, build trust, and navigate a web of regulations while dealing with highly skeptical audiences.

Sounds tough? It is. But that is exactly why storytelling is so powerful — it can help bridge these gaps.

Let us break down the unique challenge pharma marketers face and why they make storytelling both essential and tricky.

1. **The Strict Regulatory Maze**

   Unlike other industries, pharma marketing operates under tight regulations. Everything you say has to be:

   - Scientifically accurate
   - Legally compliant
   - Ethically responsible

   Regulatory agencies like the FDA (USA), EMA (Europe), and other national bodies have strict guidelines to ensure that pharmaceutical messaging is not misleading.

   The Challenge?

   Storytelling thrives on emotions and creativity, but you can't overpromise, oversimplify, or dramatize in pharmaceuticals. Even a beautifully crafted story is useless if it violates compliance.

   The Solution:

   Focus on authentic, fact-based storytelling. Use real patient stories backed by data, but without making exaggerated claims.

2. **Balancing Science with Simplicity**

Pharma brands deal with complex science — clinical trials, mechanisms of action, and intricate medical jargon. But here is the catch:

- Most patients and even some doctors don't want dense, scientific explanations.
- Overly simplified messages may be inaccurate or misleading.

The Challenge?

How do you make complex medical information engaging and understandable without dumbing it down?

The Solution:

Use metaphors and real-world analogies to simplify scientific concepts. For example:

Instead of saying:

"This medication inhibits pro-inflammatory cytokine production to reduce disease progression."

Try this:

"Think of your immune system like a defense team. Sometimes, it overreacts and attacks your own body. This drug acts like a 'calm-down' signal, helping your body regain balance."

Now, it makes sense without losing accuracy.

3. **Overcoming Distrust in Pharma**

Let us be honest — many people do not trust pharmaceutical companies. High drug prices, past controversies, and misinformation have fueled skepticism.

The Challenge?

How do you market a drug or treatment when some people already doubt your industry's intentions?

The Solution:

Authenticity and transparency. Instead of pushing promotional messages, use real patient success stories, behind-the-scenes research insights, and healthcare professionals' testimonials to build credibility.

- Show the human side of pharma — introduce the researchers who spent years developing a drug.
- Use patient advocacy stories to highlight the impact of treatments beyond just numbers.

People trust people, not faceless corporations. Put a human face on your brand.

4. **Addressing Multiple Stakeholders with Different Needs**

In most industries, your audience is straightforward — you market to customers. In pharma? Not so simple. You have to communicate with:

- Doctors & Healthcare Professionals — They want clinical data and evidence.
- Patients & Caregivers — They want easy-to-understand information and reassurance.
- Regulators & Payers — They need cost-effectiveness and compliance details.

The Challenge?

How do you create a storytelling strategy that resonates with all these different audiences?

The Solution:

Tailor your messaging for each group while keeping a consistent brand narrative.

- For Doctors — Use data-driven storytelling, patient case studies, and clinical trial success stories.
- For Patients — Share relatable, emotionally compelling patient journeys.
- For Payers & Regulators — Show real-world evidence, health economics data, and long-term benefits.

Same brand story, but adapted for different perspectives.

5. **Standing Out in an Overcrowded Market**

Every pharmaceutical company is trying to capture attention, whether through new drug launches, digital health solutions, or disease awareness campaigns.

The Challenge?

How do you differentiate your brand when competitors are telling similar stories?

The Solution:

Find your unique brand voice and focus on what makes your product, approach, or mission different.

- Maybe it's your patient-first philosophy.
- Maybe it's your cutting-edge research.
- Maybe it's your commitment to affordability or accessibility.

Example: Instead of saying, "We developed a new asthma drug," tell the story of the researchers who worked for years to create it, and how it is changing lives.

Stories are not just what you say — they are how you say it.

Final Takeaway: Turning Challenges into Opportunities

Yes, pharma marketing comes with unique hurdles, which is why storytelling is so important.

A great story can:

- Make complex science understandable
- Build trust in a skeptical industry
- Connect with different stakeholders
- Help your brand stand out in a crowded space

The key: Keep it real, keep it ethical, and always keep your audience in mind.

Because, at the end of the day, the best pharma marketing is not about selling pills — It is about telling stories that change lives.

Opportunities for Differentiation

How Storytelling Sets Your Pharma Brand Apart

Pharma marekting is a crowded space. Dozens of companies sell similar treatments, use similar messages, and target the same audience. So, how do you stand out?

The answer: Storytelling.

Storytelling is not just about making your brand sound interesting. It is about making it memorable, relatable, and different from the sea of sameness. When done right, storytelling can transform your pharmaceutical brand from just another name into something that resonates, inspires trust, and connects with people on a human level.

Let us explore how storytelling can differentiate your brand and create a lasting impact.

1. **Tell Stories That Go Beyond the Science**

   Pharma marketing often focuses on scientific data, efficacy rates, and clinical trial results — and while these are essential, they don't always connect with your audience emotionally.

   The differentiation Opportunity?

   Move beyond just the science and tell the human stories behind the medicine.

   - Showcase the researchers who worked tirelessly to develop the treatment.
   - Highlight the patients whose lives have been changed.
   - Tell the story of the problem, not just the solution — why was this treatment needed in the first place?

   Example: Instead of saying:

   "Our drug reduces migraine frequency by 60%."

   Try:

   "Meet Sarah. She used to miss important family moments due to debilitating migraines. Today, thanks to [your drug], she is reclaiming her life."

The second version is not just informative — It's emotional, relatable, and memorable.

2. **Leverage Your Brand's Unique Purpose**

   Every pharma company has products. But what is your mission? What is your deeper "why"?

   The Differentiation Opportunity?

   Find your brand's bigger purpose and weave it into your storytelling.

   - Are you committed to making life-saving affordable?
   - Are you investing in rare disease research that others overlook?
   - Are you revolutionizing patient care with digital health innovations?

   Example:

   Think about Johnson & Johnson's long-standing focus on caregivers. Instead of just selling medical products, they tell stories about the parents, nurses, and doctors who use them. That focus on human care sets them apart.

   What is your company's bigger story? Find it, tell it, and own it.

3. **Personalization: Make Stories Feel Tailored**

   One-size-fits-all messaging is boring. People don't want generic stories — they want stories that feel relevant to them.

   The Differentiation Opportunity?

   Use personalized storytelling to speak directly to different audiences.

   - For doctors? Share a case study of how your treatment helped a patient in their specialty.
   - For patients, feature real people who overcame challenges with your product.
   - For payers? Show data-driven success stories that prove cost-effectiveness.

Example: Instead of running one generic ad for a diabetes treatment, create multiple version**s:**

- For a young patient: A story about staying active and social
- For an older patient: A story about managing diabetes while enjoying retirement.
- For a doctor: A story about improved patient adherence and outcomes

Tailored storytelling = better engagement = stronger brand differentiation.

4. **Use Digital & AI-Powered Storytelling**

The way we tell stories is evolving. Traditional ads and brochures are no longer enough; interactive, AI-powered, and digital storytelling is changing the game.

The Differentiation Opportunity?

Use cutting-edge storytelling formats to engage audiences in new ways.

- AI-generated patient narratives that adapt based on user interactions.
- Augmented reality (AR) and virtual reality (VR) to visualize drug mechanisms.
- Gamification — turn medical education into interactive storytelling experiences.

Example:

Some pharmaceutical companies are using VR to simulate life for patients with diseases like Alzheimer's or Parkinson's. This immersive storytelling creates deep empathy and understanding, making your brand unforgettable.

5. **Engage in Authentic, Two-Way Storytelling**

Marketing used to be one-way: companies spoke, and the audience listened. Not anymore.

Today, the most powerful storytelling happens when brands engage in real conversations with their audiences.

The Differentiation Opportunity?

Turn storytelling into a two-way dialogue — let patients, doctors, and caregivers be part of the story.

- Encourage user-generated content — let patients share their own experiences.
- Host interactive webinars or live Q&As where real people tell their stories.
- Use social media storytelling — feature patient advocacy groups and healthcare professionals.

Example:

Some pharma brands have created patient storytelling platforms where real people share their treatment journeys. This approach fosters trust, credibility, and deeper connections.

The Bottom Line: Stand Out With Stories That Matter

Pharma marketing is full of regulations, data, and technical details. But what truly differentiates brands is not what they sell—it's the stories they tell.

- Go beyond the science — bring in the human element.
- Find your brand's deeper purpose — and make it part of your narrative.
- Personalize your stories — speak directly to each audience.
- Embrace new formats — AI, VR, gamification, and interactive content.
- Create conversations, not just messages — engage your audience.

At the end of the day, pharmaceuticals are not just about drugs. They are about hope, healing, and human lives. The brands that tell those stories best will be the ones that truly stand out.

Part II. The History and Evolution of Storytelling

When you think about storytelling in pharma, it might seem like a pretty modern concept — something tied to slick ad campaigns or patient videos on Instagram. But if you dig a little deeper, you'll find that storytelling has been part of healthcare communication for much longer than expected. It just looked very different at first.

In the early days of the pharmaceutical industry, communication was all about data, data, data. Think clinical trial results, dense product brochures, and long-winded presentations packed with technical jargon. The focus was purely on science, which made sense because trust had to be built through evidence. The story was: "Here's the proof that this works."

No emotion. No personal connection. Just hard facts.

But over time, something shifted.

Marketers — and even healthcare providers — realized that people don't make decisions based on facts alone. Even physicians, who are trained to be objective, are still human. Patients certainly are. Everyone responds better to communication that feels personal, relatable, and meaningful.

The real turning point came when pharmaceutical companies realized that selling a product is not enough—they must also tell the human story behind the product.

Instead of talking at people with clinical data, brands began sharing real stories:

- A patient who got their life back thanks to a breakthrough medication.
- A caregiver who found hope through a new treatment.
- A physician who fought to get access to the latest therapies for their patients.

By the 2000s, storytelling exploded with the rise of patient advocacy groups, direct-to-consumer advertising (especially in places like the U.S.), and later social media. Pharma companies realized they could build relationships, not just transactions. A well-told patient story could move people far more deeply than a list of clinical endpoints ever could.

And then came technology—YouTube videos, podcasts, Instagram stories, virtual reality experiences—opening up endless new ways to tell stories that immersed audiences emotionally while complying with strict regulations.

Today, storytelling in pharma is patient-centric, authentic, multi-channel, and highly strategic.

It's about shining a light on the why behind treatments. It's about putting the patient, not the pill, at the center. It's about making science human.

In short, storytelling in pharmaceuticals has evolved from an afterthought to one of the most powerful tools for building trust, inspiring hope, and driving meaningful engagement. And the journey is only just beginning.

CHAPTER

4

The Origins of Storytelling

Let's rewind — way, way back — to the very beginning.

Before there were books, before there were written languages, before even formal medicine as we know it... There were stories.

Sitting around campfires, ancient humans shared tales of survival, healing, danger, and hope. These weren't just for entertainment (though no doubt a little drama made them more memorable!). Stories were how knowledge was passed down, how cultures survived, how lessons were learned.

Think about it: if you're trying to teach your community about a deadly plant or a miraculous healing herb, you could either list facts or tell a vivid story about the brave healer who saved a life. Guess which one people remembered?

Storytelling was — and still is — humanity's oldest form of communication.

It's hardwired into our brains. Neuroscience even shows that when we hear a story, our brains release oxytocin — the "feel-good" chemical that builds trust and emotional connection. It's like stories are a biological language of their own.

Fast forward to early civilizations — ancient Egypt, Greece, India, and China — and you find rich traditions of storytelling woven into medicine, philosophy, and healing practices.

From Homer's epics to Ayurveda's ancient teachings, knowledge wasn't just shared through dry instruction; it was wrapped in narrative. Heroes faced challenges, wise healers offered remedies, and the triumph of life over death was a common thread.

In short:

- Storytelling started as a survival tool.
- It evolved into a way of teaching, healing, and inspiring.
- And today, even in our hyper-digital world, it remains the most powerful way to connect with others, heart to heart, mind to mind.

When we tell stories, we're tapping into something timeless and universal.

It's not just communication.

It's a human connection at its purest.

Storytelling Across Cultures and Time

Let's travel back in time to see how storytelling has evolved and how it has become a game-changer in pharmaceutical marketing.

1. **The Origins of Storytelling: Myths, Legends, and Oral Traditions**

   Before books, there were stories passed down by word of mouth. Ancient cultures used storytelling to explain the mysteries of the world, pass on traditions, and shape their identities.

   Early Storytelling Forms:

   - Cave paintings (as old as 30,000 years) depicted stories of hunts and rituals.
   - Oral traditions kept history alive — people memorized and performed epic tales before writing.
   - Myths and legends helped societies make sense of life, death, and the unknown.

   Example: The ancient Indian epic Mahabharata, one of the longest stories ever written, was passed down orally for centuries before being recorded in text.

   Even today, we still love stories of heroes, challenges, and triumphs — because they speak to something universal in all of us.

2. **The Rise of Written Storytelling: From Scrolls to Print**

   As civilizations advanced, so did storytelling. The invention of writing allowed stories to be recorded, preserved, and shared across generations.

   Key milestones in written storytelling:

   - Clay tablets and scrolls (Sumerians, Egyptians, and Greeks recorded myths and history).

- The invention of paper and books made storytelling more accessible.
- The printing press (15th century) revolutionized how stories were distributed.

  Example: In the 1700s and 1800s, newspapers and books allowed companies to start crafting brand stories, marking the birth of advertising storytelling.

  Now, brands do not just sell products—they tell stories about who they are and what they stand for.

3. **The Evolution of Storytelling in Marketing**

Marketing and storytelling have always gone hand in hand. Think about it — what's a brand if not a story?

Key milestones and shifts in marketing:

- 19th-century print ads began to use storytelling to build trust and credibility.
- 10th-century radio and TV commercials used stories to create emotional connections.
- Late 20th century: Brands like Apple, Nike, and Coca-Cola mastered brand storytelling.

Example:

- Coca-Cola's "Share a Coke" campaign didn't just sell soda — it told stories about friendship, happiness, and connection by putting real names on bottles.
- By the 21st century, brands realized something crucial: People don't just buy products — they buy into stories.

4. **Storytelling in Pharma: From Data to Emotion**

Pharma marketing, for a long time, was dominated by science, numbers, and clinical claims. But that was never enough — because while data informs, stories persuade.

How storytelling changed pharma marketing:

- Early pharma ads (1900s): Focused on technical details and medical claims.
- Mid-20th century: Brands started using testimonials and doctor endorsements.
- Late 20th century: Patient-centric stories emerged — real people, real impact.
- Digital age: Pharma storytelling became interactive, multimedia-driven, and emotionally engaging.

Example:

Dove's "Real Beauty" campaign is one of the most powerful pharmaceutical stories. Although Dove is not a pharmaceutical product, it is a healthcare-related brand that revolutionized marketing by telling authentic, human-centric stories.

5. **The Digital Revolution: The Future of Storytelling in Pharma:**

Today, storytelling is more dynamic than ever. Technology has transformed how stories are told, allowing pharma brands to connect with audiences in ways never before possible.

Modern pharma storytelling techniques:

- Social media stories and patient advocacy campaigns
- Augmented reality (AR) and virtual reality (VR) experiences
- AI-driven personalized storytelling (tailoring content to individuals)
- Gamification and interactive storytelling

Example: Companies now use virtual reality to show what life is like for patients with conditions like Alzheimer's and Parkinson's. This creates deep empathy and understanding, making the brand's message unforgettable.

The Takeaway: Pharma Storytelling Has Come Full Circle

From ancient myths to modern digital campaigns, storytelling has always been about making an impact.

- In the past, we gathered around fires. Today, we gather around screens.
- Stories used to be spoken. Now, they are interactive and AI-driven.
- The core purpose remains the same: To connect, inspire, and influence.

Pharma brands that embrace storytelling don't just sell products — they build relationships, trust, and loyalty in a way that data alone never could.

And that's why storytelling is not just an option in pharma marketing — it's the future.

Oral Traditions, Myths, and Legends

Imagine living thousands of years ago in a world without books, the internet, and social media. How would you learn about your ancestors? How would you pass down knowledge about survival, morality, or the mysteries of the universe?

The answer? Oral storytelling.

Long before we wrote anything down, humans shared stories by speaking, singing, and performing. These stories — myths, legends, or folktales — were not just entertainment. They were the lifeblood of culture, history, and identity.

The Power of Oral Traditions: Passing Stories Through Generations

Before writing existed, stories had to be memorized and passed down. And here's the incredible part: they survived for centuries, sometimes even millennia, without being written down!

Why did oral traditions work so well?

- They used repetition and rhythm to make stories easy to remember.
- They relied on vivid imagery and emotion, making them engaging.
- They were performed with music, gestures, and drama, making them immersive.

Example: The Mahabharata and the Odyssey, two of the world's greatest epics, were originally passed down orally for generations before being written.

Oral traditions were not just for fun. They helped preserve knowledge, morals, and culture in a time when forgetting a story meant losing it forever.

Myths: Stories That Explain the World

Have you ever wondered why the Sun rises or where humans came from? Ancient myths were humanity's first science. They explained natural phenomena, human nature, and even the afterlife.

What makes a myth?

- It often features gods, supernatural beings, or cosmic events.
- It explains something fundamental about life, nature, or the universe.
- It's deeply rooted in culture and belief systems.

Example: The Greek myth Prometheus tells how he stole fire from the gods and gave it to humans, explaining the origin of fire and the consequences of defying authority.

Today, myths may not be taken literally, but their themes still resonate. Superhero movies, fantasy novels, and even brand stories borrow from ancient myths!

Legends: A Blend of Truth and Fantasy

While myths explain the world, legends focus on extraordinary people and events. Some are based on real history, and some are exaggerated over time.

What makes a legend?

- It often features a hero, a great battle, or a quest.
- It's rooted in some historical truth, but details get exaggerated.
- It inspires people with tales of bravery, wisdom, or perseverance.

Example: King Arthur and his knights—were they real? Maybe. Over the centuries, his story grew into a legendary saga of honor, chivalry, and destiny.

In a way, modern marketing borrows from legends. Pharma brands, for example, often highlight pioneering scientists or breakthrough discoveries, shaping them into inspiring narratives.

The Legacy of Ancient Storytelling in Pharma Marketing

What do myths and legends have to do with pharma marketing? More than you think!

- Oral Storytelling — Word-of-mouth marketing (People trust stories told by real people!)
- Myths — Brand origin stories (How a company was founded and its "mission" often has myth-like elements.)
- Legends — Patient or scientist stories (Groundbreaking discoveries become legendary over time.)

Example: The story of Alexander Fleming's accidental discovery of penicillin has become legendary in the medical world — an example of how some of the greatest innovations happen by chance.

From Firelit Tales to Digital Screens

The way we tell stories has changed — from oral traditions to books and digital content — but the essence remains the same.

Humans crave stories that explain, inspire, and connect. Whether a village elder shares wisdom, a blockbuster movie tells a hero's journey, or a pharmaceutical brand uses patient narratives to build trust, storytelling is timeless.

So, the next time you hear a powerful brand story or compelling ad campaign, remember that it's just the modern version of myths and legends passed down through new-age storytellers.

CHAPTER

5

The Evolution of Storytelling in Pharma Marketing

From Ancient Markets to Digital Masterpieces

Imagine you are in a bustling marketplace in ancient Greece. Merchants shout, trying to sell their goods. One of them, however, is not just yelling about prices—he is telling a story.

"This Olive oil? It's from the sacred groves of Olympia, pressed by hand by my family for generations. Even the great warriors of Sparta use it for strength!"

The merchant out-marketed everyone else. Why? Because he didn't just sell a product — he sold a story. And that's the secret of marketing that has stood the test of time>

Let's explore how storytelling in marketing has evolved from ancient times to today's AI-driven narratives.

1. **The Age of Oral Storytelling (Pre-Printing Press, Before the 1400s)**

   Long before advertising as we know it, businesses relied on word-of-mouth marketing—literally.

   How did it work?

   - Merchants would tell compelling origin stories about their products.

- Symbols and simple visual storytelling (like carvings or colors) helped establish identity.
- Reputation was everything — so stories spread person-to-person like ancient viral marketing!

Example: In ancient Rome, a winemaker might tell customers, "This wine was made from grapes kissed by the same Sun that warms the Emperor's vineyards." And just like that, a premium brand was born!

2. The Printed Revolution (1400s – 1900s): The Birth of Advertisements

Then came the printing press, and storytelling in marketing scaled up massively.

What has changed?

- Printed ads emerged, filled with persuasive narratives.
- Brands started using consistent themes and slogans to craft an identity.
- Storytelling moved from one-to-one (spoken) to one-to-many (printed media).

Example: In the 1800s, snake oil salesmen used dramatic newspaper ads to tell exaggerated tales of miracle cures—an early (and sometimes unethical) example of storytelling in pharmaceutical marketing!

Meanwhile, in the 1880s, Coca-Cola did not just advertise a drink. It created a lifestyle narrative, positioning Coke as the refreshing choice in an exciting modern world.

3. The Golden Age of Brand Storytelling (1900s – 2000s): Radio, TV, and Emotional Narratives

With the rise of radio and television, storytelling in marketing became bigger, bolder, and more emotional.

How did storytelling evolve?

- Emotions took center stage — brands realized that feeling sells more than facts.

- Characters and mascots (like the Marlboro Man and Ronald McDonald) became living brand stories.
- Jingles and taglines turned brand messaging into cultural moments.

Example: Nike's "Just Do It" campaign was not just about shoes — it was about overcoming challenges, believing in yourself, and pushing limits. It transformed Nike from a sneaker company into a symbol of human potential.

Pharma marketing also evolved, with companies using patient stories to explain the impact of medicines rather than just listing medical facts.

4. **The Digital Revolution (2000s — 2010s): Interactive and Personalized Storytelling**

   Then came the Internet, and suddenly, everyone became a storyteller.

   What has changed?

   - Brands could engage with consumers directly through websites, blogs, and social media.
   - Two-way storytelling emerged — customers shared their own stories (testimonials, reviews).
   - Brands had to be authentic and human, as consumers could fact-check everything instantly.

Example: Dove's "Real Beauty" campaign featured real women, not airbrushed models. It sparked conversations about beauty standards and made the brand a champion of self-confidence.

For pharmaceuticals, storytelling became more patient-focused. Brands used videos, blogs, and testimonials to create trust and educate consumers about medical treatments.

5. **The AI and Data-Driven Era (2010s - Present): Hyper-Personalized Stories**

   Today, storytelling is smarter, faster, and more personalized than ever.

How has storytelling changed?

- AI and algorithms tailor stories to individual consumers in real time.
- Immersive experiences (AR/VR, gamification) bring brand narratives to life.
- Micro-stories on platforms like TikTok are reshaping how brands engage audiences.

Example: Pharma brands now use AI-powered chatbots to tell personalized health stories. These bots guide patients through their treatment journeys with interactive and engaging narratives.

Even wearables tech tells a story — your smartwatch does not just give you numbers; it tells the story of your health journey and encourages lifestyle changes.

The Future: Where Storytelling is Headed

Looking ahead, data-driven storytelling and AI-generated narratives will redefine how brands connect with audiences.

What's next?

- ***Predictive storytelling***: Brands will anticipate what stories you need before you even search for them.
- ***AI-generated content***: Tools like ChatGPT will help craft narratives at scale with personalization.
- ***Ethical storytelling***: As AI grows, brands must balance automation with authenticity and trust.

Final Thought: The Art of Storytelling is Timeless

From ancient merchants in the marketplace to AI-driven content today, one thing remains constant:

People do not buy products. They buy stories.

Although the tools may change, storytelling will always be at the heart of marketing. Successful brands do not just sell something—they create narratives that inspire, connect, and resonate.

And that is why storytelling in marketing will never go out of style.

Early Examples of Marketing Stories

The Birth of Brand Narratives

Let's rewind to a time before social media, before TV commercials, and even before printed ads. How did businesses convince people to buy their products? Simple: they told great stories.

From ancient marketplaces to medieval merchants, some of the earliest examples of marketing were not just about selling goods — they were about weaving compelling narratives that made products desirable, memorable, and worth talking about.

1. **The Ancient Egyptian Perfumers: Selling Mystique and Divinity**

   Imagine walking through an Egyptian market in 2000 BCE. A perfumer is not just selling scented oils — he is telling a story:

   "This fragrance is the very essence of gods, made from sacred lotus flowers plucked at dawn along the Nile. Pharaoh himself wears this scent before meeting the deities in the afterlife."

   Why did it work?

   - It created exclusivity — only the elite and divine could wear it.
   - It added an emotional and mystical connection.
   - It made the product more than a scent — a symbol of status. And divine.

   Does this sound familiar? Modern luxury brands do the same thing today—think Chanel No 5 or Tom Ford fragrances that sell an experience, not just a perfume.

2. **The Silk Road Traders: The First Influencer Marketers**

   Fast forward to the days of the Silk Road, where traders carried spices, silks, and gems across continents. These merchants were not just selling exotic goods — they were crafting irresistible tales.

"This silk? It comes from a secret valley in China where the Emperor's own weavers spin threads from the most delicate cocoons. Only a few bolts of this fabric ever leave the kingdom!

Why did it work?

- It turned an ordinary fabric into a legendary treasure.
- It made the buyer feel special, almost like they were part of a secret society.
- It used scarcity as a powerful motivator.

This tactic is alive and well today. Think Rolex ("hand-assembled and crafted with precision) or "limited-edition sneakers" (only 500 pairs available worldwide).

3. **The Roman Gladiator Endorsements: Ancient Celebrity Marketing**

In ancient Rome, gladiators were not just fighters; they were superstars. Merchants leveraged their fame to market everything from oils to armor.

A famous gladiator might be paid (or gifted) to say:

"I only use Maximus-brand olive oil before every battle. It keeps my muscles strong and my skin resilient."

Why it worked:

- It associated the product with strength and victory.
- It made ordinary Romans want to use the same oil as their heroes.
- It was one of the earliest examples of celebrity endorsements!

This is the same formula behind today's sports endorsements — whether it's Michael Jordan with Nike or Serena Williams with Gatorade.

4. **The Medieval Blacksmiths: The Power of Craftsmanship Stories**

In 14th-century Europe, blacksmiths did not just forge swords and armor — they built brand stories.

A blacksmith might say:

"This blade was forged in the fires of my great-grandfather's anvil, using techniques passed down for three generations. It's not just a sword — It's a legacy."

Why did it work?

- It added a heritage and craftsmanship angle.
- It built trust — if the technique worked for three generations, it must be good!
- It made the sword feel unique and personal.

Modern brands like Swiss watches, Italian leather goods, and Japanese samurai knives still use heritage-based storytelling to justify premium pricing.

5. **The Apothecaries and the Birth of Pharma Marketing**

Even early medicine sellers understood the value of a good story. An apothecary in the 1600s might promote a tonic by saying:

"This elixir was discovered in the mountains of Persia, where the locals live to be over 100 years old. Drink this daily, and you, too, will enjoy a long and vigorous life!"

Why it worked:

- It leveraged the power of mystery and exotic origins.
- It played on desire (a longer life) and fear (aging and illness).
- It built trust through association with long-living people.

This storytelling formula is still common in health and wellness marketing today — think of supplements that boast "ancient herbal secrets" or skincare brands promising "timeless beauty."

The Common Thread: Storytelling Sells

What do all these examples have in common?

- They did not just sell products — they sold narratives.

- They made buyers feel like they were part of something bigger.
- They tapped into emotions, whether it was exclusivity, trust, or aspiration.

And guess what? We still use these same storytelling techniques today, whether it's luxury branding, influencer marketing, or pharmaceutical storytelling.

The tools have changed, but the power of a great story remains timeless.

The Rise of Brand Narratives

From Selling Products to Telling Stories

Let's take a journey back in time. Once upon a time, marketing was simple: "Here is a product. It's great. Buy it."

That was it. No emotions, no connection, no deeper meaning. Just a straightforward transaction.

But something changed. Companies started realizing that people don't just buy products — they buy into stories, identities, and emotions. And just like that, the age of brand narratives was born.

The Shift: From Features to Feelings

In the early days of advertising, brands focused purely on features and benefits.

- "This radio has the best frequency range!"
- "This car has the most powerful engine!"
- "This soap will clean your hands better than any other!"

Logical? Yes.

Persuasive? Not always.

The problem? Facts alone don't sell — because humans don't make decisions purely based on logic. We are emotional creatures.

So, brands shifted their focus from "what our product does" to "how our product makes you feel."

Coca-Cola: Selling Happiness, not Soda

Think Coca-Cola, for example.

In the 1950s, Coke ads used to focus on the product:

"Refreshing! Ice-cold Coca-Cola!"

But in the 1970s, something changed. The brand started selling an experience.

Remember the legendary "I'd Like to Buy the World a Coke" ad? It did not mention the taste of Coke. Instead, it showed people coming together, singing in harmony, sharing a Coke, and spreading joy.

Suddenly, Coke was not just a drink — it was a symbol of happiness, unity, and friendship.

And that's when the power of brand narratives took off.

Nike: More Than Just Sneakers

Nike does not sell shoes. It sells inspiration.

Its legendary slogan, "Just Do It," is not about sneakers. It is about:

- Pushing past limits
- Overcoming self-doubt
- Becoming the best version of yourself

Nike tells stories of:

- Athletes defying the odds
- Everyday people pushing themselves
- Legends who refuse to give up

The product? It's just the supporting character. The real hero of Nike's story? YOU.

Apple: The Art of Belonging

Apple does not sell computers and phones. It sells a movement.

Think back to their iconic "Think Different" campaign. It featured:

- Mahatma Gandhi
- Pablo Picasso
- Albert Einstein

What was the message? Apple is not just for tech geeks. It's for rebels, visionaries, and creative thinkers.

And suddenly, buying an Apple product was not just a purchase but a statement.

How Brand Narratives Took Over Pharma Marketing

Now, let's bring it into pharma marketing.

For decades, pharma marketing was purely factual.

- "This drug has a 75% success rate."
- "This therapy reduces symptoms by 40%."
- "Clinically tested. FDA-approved."

Of course, those things are essential, but something was missing: the human element.

The shift began when pharmaceutical companies started telling patient stories.

Instead of just talking about efficacy rates, they showcased:

- A mother regaining her strength after chemotherapy.
- A child managing diabetes and playing soccer again.
- A grandfather getting back to gardening after a heart procedure.

The message? This is not just medicine. This is giving people their lives back.

The New Era of Brand Narratives

Today, every successful brand—whether in food, tech, fashion, or pharmaceuticals—has a narrative.

It's no longer about what you sell.

It's about why you sell it.

Brand storytelling turns products into experiences, companies into movements, and customers into loyal communities.

The best part? When done right, storytelling makes people buy your product and believe in it.

Case Studies from Non-Pharmaceutical Sectors

Storytelling is not just a tool — it's the heart of branding. Some of the world's most successful companies have used storytelling to build empires, create loyal followings, and make their products unforgettable.

Let's explore how these non-pharma giants —Airbnb, Patagonia, and Dove — have mastered storytelling and what pharma marketers can learn from them.

1. **Airbnb: Selling Belongings, Not Just Stays**

   Imagine you are planning a trip. You could book a hotel — a standard, predictable room. Or you could stay in a charming home with a personal touch, experience the culture like a local, and create memories.

   That's the magic Airbnb tapped into.

   Instead of marketing itself as another accommodation service, Airbnb built its entire brand around the powerful human emotion of belonging.

   How They Did It:

   - User-generated stories — Real travelers share their personal Airbnb experiences.
   - Emotional messaging — Their tagline, "Belong Anywhere," focuses on connection, not transactions.
   - Compelling visuals — Their marketing is not about properties; it's about experiences —laughter over dinner, exploring new cities, forming friendships.

   Impact: Airbnb transformed the travel industry by making every guest feel like a local. Its storytelling made it more than just a booking platform—it became a community.

   Lesson for Pharma:

   Pharma brands should not just talk about their products. They should tell patient stories — how a treatment helped someone reclaim their life, achieve their dreams, or feel like themselves again.

2. **Patagonia: Fighting for a Cause, Not Just Selling Jackets**

   Most companies sell products. Patagonia sells a movement.

   This outdoor clothing brand could have focused on technical specs—waterproof materials, durability, and insulation—but instead, it built a story around environmental activism.

   How They Did It:

   - Cause-driven storytelling – Patagonia champions sustainability, climate action, and ethical production.
   - Daring campaigns – in 2011, they launched the infamous "Don't Buy This Jacket" ad, urging customers to buy less to reduce waste.
   - Authenticity – The company donates 1% of sales to environmental causes and supports grassroots activism.

Impact: Patagonia's story resonates with environmentally conscious consumers. People don't just buy their clothes; they buy into their mission.

Lesson for Pharma: In a world where trust in pharmaceuticals is often shaky, brands must stand for something more than profit. Whether it is patient advocacy, access to medicine, or healthcare education, pharma companies should craft narratives that align with meaningful missions.

3. **Dove: Redefining Beauty with Emotional Storytelling**

   Beauty ads traditionally featured flawless supermodels. Then, Dove flipped the script.

   Instead of airbrushed perfection, Dove's "Real Beauty" campaign celebrated everyday women of all shapes, sizes, and ages.

   How They Did It:

   - Authentic representation – Real women, not models, in ads.
   - Emotional Storytelling: The viral "Dove Real Beauty Sketches" ad showed women describing themselves rather than how others saw them, revealing a powerful truth about self-perception.

- Social impact — Dove launched programs to boost self-esteem among young girls.

Impact: Dove did not just sell soap. It started a global conversation about beauty standards and made consumers feel seen and valued.

Lesson for Pharma: Healthcare is not just about treating diseases; it's about empowering people. Pharma brands can humanize their messaging by telling stories that focus on confidence, resilience, and quality of life.

Key Takeaways: What Pharma Can Learn

- Make it about people, not products — Tell human stories that connect emotionally.
- Align with a purpose — Stand for something bigger than just selling medicine.
- Use real voices — Feature patients, caregivers, and doctors sharing authentic experiences.
- Create a movement — Build a community around shared values and trust.

In pharma marketing, the power of storytelling is not just a nice-to-have — it's the key to making an impact that lasts.

CHAPTER

6

Storytelling in Pharma: A Historical Perspective

Storytelling has always been a part of medicine, long before pharmaceutical companies existed. Before clinical trials and data-driven marketing, healing was passed down through stories. Shamans, healers, and ancient physicians used narratives to explain diseases, remedies, and the power of healing herbs.

Fast-forward to today, and while the science of medicine has advanced, the role of storytelling in pharmaceuticals remains just as powerful. Let's journey through time to see how storytelling in pharmaceuticals has evolved and why it is more important than ever.

1. **The Earliest Forms of Medical Storytelling**

   Before the rise of modern medicine, healing was rooted in oral traditions. People believed in remedies passed down through generations, often wrapped in myths and fables.

   Ancient Egypt & Greece: Physicians like Imhotep and Hippocrates practiced medicine and wrote about it, telling stories of patient recoveries and the philosophy of healing.

   Traditional Chinese Medicine (TCM): Healing practices were shared through parables, describing the balance of Yin and Yang and the importance of harmony.

Lesson for Pharma: Even before science proved the effectiveness of medicine, people trusted it because of stories that made it relatable and understandable.

2. **The Rise of Pharma Marketing and Patient Narratives**

In the early 20th century, pharmaceutical marketing was heavily product-focused. Companies relied on medical representatives to share facts and figures with doctors rather than engaging in storytelling.

But something changed. Pharma brands began to realize that facts alone were not enough. They needed stories to humanize their medicines.

1950s – The Birth of Brand Storytelling

Big names like Pfizer, Merck, and Eli Lilly started running newspaper advertisements, sharing testimonials from doctors and patients. These advertisements were not just about efficacy—they addressed the real-life impact of medicines.

1980s– The Power of Television and Direct-to-Consumer (DTC) Storytelling

As regulators on advertising relaxed in the US, pharma brands embraced TV commercials. Instead of just listing side effects, brands began showcasing patient journeys – before and after taking a medicine.

Example: The launch of antidepressants like Prozac featured stories of people reclaiming their lives from depression, making mental health conversations mainstream.

Lesson for Pharma: When patients see someone like them overcoming a health challenge, they are more likely to trust and engage with a brand.

3. **The Digital Era and Patient-Centric Storytelling**

   The Internet changed everything. Patients no longer relied solely on doctors for information. They started searching online, joining health forums, and sharing their experiences.

   2000s – Social Media and the Rise of Patient Advocacy

   Patients shared their health journeys on Facebook, YouTube, and blogs, and pharmaceutical companies saw an opportunity to market their products and participate in these conversations.

   Example: GSK's "More Than COPD" campaign shared real patient stories to raise awareness and inspire those with the disease.

   2010s –The Era of Empathy-Driven Campaigns

   Pharma brands moved away from traditional ads and leaned into emotional storytelling.

   Example: Novartis' "Heart Failure: A Story of Survival" followed the real-life journey of a patient, making the condition personal rather than just medical.

   Lesson for Pharma: People trust people, not brands. Pharma marketing shifted from talking about products to elevating real patient voices.

4. **The Future: AI, Personalization, and Interactive Storytelling**

   With AI and data-driven storytelling, pharma companies can now craft personalized narratives.

   - **Wearable Tech and Personalized Stories:** Smart Devices track patient health, allowing pharmaceutical brands to create custom stories around real-time data.
   - **AI-Generated Content:** AI can now craft individualized health journeys, adapting stories based on a patient's behavior and medical history.

- **Virtual Reality (VR) and augmented Reality (AR):** Imagine patients experiencing their treatment journey through immersive storytelling instead of just reading about it.

Lesson for Pharma: The next era of storytelling will be about deep personalization, making every patient feel seen, heard, and understood.

Final Thoughts: Why Pharma Must Keep Telling Stories

Pharma marketing has come full circle — from word-of-mouth in ancient times to AI-driven storytelling today. But the core remains the same: stories build trust.

As science continues to evolve, pharmaceutical brands that focus on real human stories rather than just data will be the ones that truly connect with patients, doctors, and caregivers.

Because, at the end of the day, people don't remember facts – they remember stories.

How Pharma Started Using Stories

From Pills to People

Pharmaceutical companies were not always storytellers. In the early days, their marketing was purely scientific, focused on chemical compositions, clinical studies, and hard data. Ads looked like text-heavy medical journals, full of dense explanations that only doctors could understand.

But here is the thing: facts alone don't move people. Stories do.

Pharma companies eventually realized that patients and doctors do not just buy medicine – they buy hope, relief, and a better quality of life. And the best way to communicate that? Through stories.

1. **The Early Days: When Pharma Spoke to Doctors, Not Patients**

   In the early 1900s, pharma companies primarily marketed to physicians. The logic was simple:

   - Doctors prescribe, so let's convince them first.

   Back then, pharmaceutical ads were dry, clinical, and looked like mini research papers. They focused on efficacy, dosage, and safety profiles—all essential but not exactly engaging.

   Example: An aspirin ad from the early 20th century might read:

   "Acetylsalicylic acid inhibits cyclooxygenase enzymes, reducing inflammation and fever."

   Useful? Yes.

   Memorable? Not really.

   These ads did not tell why aspirin mattered to a patient suffering from chronic pain. There was no emotional connection.

2. **The Shift: Realizing That People Trust Stories More Than Science Alone**

   By the mid-20th century, pharmaceutical companies started noticing something interesting:

- When they shared stories of patients who benefited from a drug, doctors were more likely to remember and prescribe it.

This marked a turning point. Instead of relying solely on scientific data, companies began using stories to bring medicines to life.

Example – The 1950s and The Rise of Patient Testimonials

Instead of just explaining how insulin worked, ads started sharing patient journeys:

- A diabetic child able to play outside again thanks to insulin.
- A father who regained his energy to spend time with his family.

By attaching real-world emotions to treatments, pharma companies ies humanized medicine for the first time.

3. **The Power of Emotions: From Silent Pills to Loud Stories**

The 1960s—1980s saw another evolution: storytelling was not just about the drug's effect but about the bigger impact on life.

TV and Print Ads Focused on Empathy

Instead of just saying, "This pill reduces cholesterol," ads started saying:

"This pill helps you stay healthy so you can dance at your daughter's wedding."

Example: The First Direct-to-Consumer (DTC) ADs

In the 1980s, pharma marketing took a huge leap: the FDA allowed Direct-to-Consumer (DTC) advertising.

- Now, patients were not just hearing about drugs from doctors – they were seeing them on TV.
- Stories became more personal, focusing on how medications improved daily life.

Pharma storytelling had officially shifted from doctors to patients.

4. **The Modern Era: The Rise of Digital & Patient-Led Narratives**

   The Internet and social media have transformed storytelling. Patients could now share their stories, and pharmaceutical brands had to listen.

   2000s — Online Patient Communities

   Patients began forming support groups and forums to discuss their experiences with medications. Instead of pharma companies telling stories, patients were now creating them.

   Example — GSK's More Than COPD Campaign.

   Pharma brands began embracing social media, featuring:

   - Patient interviews
   - Doctor insights in layman's terms
   - Behind-the-scenes R&D stores

   These stories made pharma companies feel more human and built trust.

5. **The Future: Personalized & AI-Driven Storytelling**

   Pharma storytelling is now heading into an even more personalized era:

   - AI-powered patient stories based on real data
   - VR & AR experiences showing inside-the-body transformations
   - Chatbots that offer real-time, empathy-driven medical guidance

   One thing is clear: pharma can't go back to the days of just listing clinical data. The brands that win hearts will be those that tell authentic, meaningful stories.

   Because, at the end of the day, medicine is not just about molecules — It's about people.

The Evolution of Patient-Centric Narratives

From Data to Humanity

If you rewind a few decades, pharmaceutical marketing was almost entirely focused on science, statistics, and doctors. The messaging was directed at healthcare professionals and filled with technical jargon about efficacy rates and clinical trials. Patients? They were passive recipients, simply taking what their doctors prescribed without much say in the matter.

But then, something remarkable happened—patients started becoming the heroes of their healthcare journeys, and pharmaceutical marketing had to evolve.

1. **The Early Days: When Patients Were Barely in the Picture**

   For most of the 20th century, pharma marketing followed a doctor-first approach. The idea was simple:

   - Convince the doctor – Doctor prescribes the drug – Patient takes it, no questions asked
   - Ads looked like medical textbooks, featuring graphs, statistics, and complex chemical explanations. Patients who saw one of these ads would probably feel like they were reading a science experiment rather than something that could improve their lives.

   Example – An Old Aspirin Ad (1920s):

   "Clinically proven to reduce pyrexia and inhibit prostaglandin synthesis."

   Translation? It helps with fever and pain relief, but the ad was not speaking to the person in pain – it was speaking to doctors.

   Patients were not at the center of the story. In fact, they were not even in the story.

2. **The Shift Begins: Patient Testimonials and Real-Life Experiences (1950s-1980s)**

   By the mid-20th century, pharmaceutical companies realized something important :

   - People don't just want to hear about a drug's mechanism of action — they want to know how it changes lives.

   So, storytelling began shifting toward real patient experiences. Instead of focusing purely on scientific claims, brands started featuring human emotions and real-world benefits.

   Example— The First TV Ads (1960s)

   Instead of saying:

   "The pill reduces cholesterol."

   Ads started saying:

   "Now you can keep up with your grandkids without worrying about heart disease."

   For the first time, the patient became the focal point. The story was no longer about the pill but about the person taking it.

3. **The Rise of Direct-to-COnsumer (DTC) Advertising (1980s-1990s)**

   A major turning point came in 1985 when the FDA allowed direct-to-consumer (DTC) advertising.

   Suddenly, pharma companies did not just have to convince doctors — they had to speak directly to patients.

   This changed everything.

   - Instead of talking about "products," ads started telling patient success stories.
   - Instead of complex medical terms, they used relatable, everyday language.
   - Instead of just targeting physicians, they targeted people watching TV at home.

Example— Prozac (1990s): The Story of Hope

Before antidepressants were openly discussed, depression was often seen as a personal weakness rather than a medical condition.

- When Prozac entered the market, its marketing campaign shifted the narrative:

"You are not alone. Millions suffer from depression, but there is hope. Prozac can help you reclaim your life."

- Patients were not just statistics anymore.
- The message was not just about reducing symptoms — it was about getting your life back.

This emotional, patient-first storytelling approach resonated deeply, paving the way for more personal, humanized pharma narratives.

4. **The Internet Revolution: Patients Start Owning Their Stories (2000s-2010s)**

With the rise of the Internet, online forums, and social media, something incredible happened:

- Patients started telling their own stories.

Before, pharma companies controlled the patient narrative. Now, patients have a platform to share their real, unfiltered experiences with diseases, treatments, and medications.

Online Patient Communities (2000s)

- Platforms like PatientsLikeMe, Inspire, and WebMD forums allowed patients to share their experiences with others.
- Patients were no longer just listening to pharmaceutical ads—they were talking back, discussing side effects, treatment challenges, and success stories.

Social Media Storytelling (2010s)

- Pharma companies began collaborating with real patients to tell authentic stories.
- They used videos, blogs, and social media testimonials to highlight how treatments were making a difference.
- Instead of scripted ads, patients were sharing their raw, personal journeys.

Example— #MoreThanMS Campaign (2016)

Multiple sclerosis (MS) patients used social media to challenge stereotypes about the disease. Instead of pharma companies telling their stories, patients themselves led the conversation, sharing videos of themselves rock climbing, running marathons, or simply living full lives despite their diagnosis.

This was a huge shift — patients were not just part of the story anymore; they were leading it.

5. **The Present & Future: Hyper-Personalized & AI-Powered Narratives (2020s & Beyond)**

Today, storytelling in pharma is more patient-centric than ever, and technology is taking it to the next level:

- **AI and Data-Driven Storytelling**
  - Pharma brands can now customize patient stories based on data.
  - AI helps create personalized content that speaks to individual patients rather than broad audiences.
- **Augmented Reality (AR) and Virtual Reality (VR) for Patient Stories**
  - VR can simulate life with a disease, helping others understand what patients go through.
  - AR can create immersive experiences showing how medications work inside the body.

- Empowered Patients as Advocates
- Today's patients don't just want to hear stories —they want to tell them/
- Pharma brands that embrace patient-driven content (via social media, video testimonials, and advocacy groups) are the ones that will build the most trust.

Example — AI-Powered Patient Support (2023)

Some pharmaceutical companies now use AI-powered chatbots that provide empathetic, human-like conversations to guide patients through their treatment journeys. These chatbots offer:

- Personalized medication reminders
- Emotional support through patient stories
- Tips and real-life testimonials from others with the same condition

This is not just storytelling — it's patient empowerment.

Final Thoughts: The Future of Patient-Centric Pharma Narratives

We have come a long way from clinical, data-heavy marketing that spoke only to doctors. Today, pharma storytelling is about:

- Empathy over expertise
- Real patient voices over scripted ads
- Hope over just hard facts

And the best part? This is not the end of the evolution — it's just the beginning.

Because, in the end, healthcare is not about prescriptions.

It's about people.

Part III. Why and How Storytelling Works in Pharma Marketing

Imagine this: You walk into a doctor's office. On the table, there are two brochures. One is filled with statistics, chemical names, and a long list of clinical trial data. The other tells the story of a real patient — let's say, Sarah — who struggled with a chronic condition, found the right treatment, and finally got her life back.

Which one are you more likely to read?

That's the power of storytelling.

Pharma marketing has long been dominated by data-heavy messaging, but here is the truth: People don't make decisions based purely on numbers — they make them based on emotions. And storytelling taps into that emotional connection in a way that pure science never can.

So, let's break it down:

- Why does storytelling work in pharma marketing?
- How can pharmaceutical companies do it effectively?
- Why Storytelling Works in Pharma Marketing

1. **Stories Make Science More Relatable**

   Pharmaceuticals are based on complex science, including molecular structures, clinical trials, and regulatory approvals. However, that complexity can overwhelm patients and even some healthcare professionals.

   A well-crafted story translates science into human experience.

   Example: Instead of saying, "This medication has a 75% efficacy rate,"

   Tell the story of John, a patient who was once unable to play with his kids due to chronic pain but now enjoys family time again because of this treatment.

   Why it works: People remember stories better than statistics. A compelling patient story can communicate the same scientific message without the medical jargon.

2. **Stories Create Emotional Connections**

   People don't just buy products — they buy hope, relief, and trust.

   - Patients facing life-changing conditions are not just looking for medication; they are looking for reassurance that they are not alone.
   - Doctors are not just looking at clinical trial data; they want to know how a drug will change their patients' lives.

   Example: A campaign for an oncology drug could feature real-life cancer survivors sharing how they reclaimed their lives post-treatment.

   Why it Works: Emotions drive decisions. When people feel something, they are more likely to trust, remember, and act.

3. **Stories Build Trust and Credibility**

   Let's be honest — pharma has had trust issues. Over-promising claims, pricing concerns, and skepticism about Big Pharma often make audiences wary.

   A well-told story — especially one rooted in real patient experiences —humanizes the brand and builds credibility.

   Example: A documentary-style video featuring real healthcare providers explaining how a drug has transformed their patients' lives.

   Why it works: Authenticity builds trust. When pharma brands tell genuine, transparent stories, people listen.

4. **Stories Influence Decision-Making**

   Neuroscience research shows that stories activate multiple parts of the brain, including the language center and the sensory and emotional regions.

   - When we hear a dry fact, only one part of the brain processes it.
   - When we hear a story, our brain immerses itself in the experience.

Example: Instead of saying, "Our medication improves lung function in COPD patients,"

Tell the story of Lisa, who went from struggling to climb stairs to hiking with her grandkids.

Why it works: People make buying and prescribing decisions based on how something makes them feel.

How to Implement Storytelling in Pharma Marketing

Now that we know why storytelling is powerful, let's discuss how pharma companies can use it effectively.

1. **Put the Patient at the Center of the Story**

   Forget about your product for a second — focus on the person whose life will change.

   - **Bad storytelling:** "Our drug is clinically proven to reduce pain by 60%."
   - **Great Storytelling:** "Mark, a marathon runner, almost gave up his dream due to his chronic pain. Thanks to this treatment, he crossed the finish line again."

   How to do it:

   - Feature real patients (with their consent).
   - Use testimonials, videos, and personal interviews.
   - Focus on quality of life, not just symptom relief.

2. **Use Doctor & Caregiver Stories**

   While patient stories are powerful, let's not forget the doctors, nurses, and caregivers who play a crucial role in treatment decisions.

   Example: A campaign featuring oncologists talking about the emotional impact of helping their patients fight cancer.

   How to do it:

   - Showcase doctor-patient relationships.
   - Highlight the human side of healthcare professionals.

- Include caregivers, because they are often key decision-makers.

3. **Use Multiple Formats for Storytelling**

   Not everyone absorbs stories the same way. Some prefer videos, others like articles, and some engage more with interactive experiences.

   - Video Stories: Mini-documentaries, patient testimonials, animated explainers.
   - Written Stories: Blog posts, articles, case studies, and interviews.
   - Interactive Experiences: Augmented Reality (AR) or Virtual Reality (VR) to show what it is like to live with a disease.

   Examples include VR experiences that simulate what it is like to have Parkinson's disease, helping caregivers and doctors experience the patient's reality.

   How to do it:

   - Choose formats based on audience preference.
   - Test different content types — what works for HCPs might not work for patients.
   - Ensure the story is accessible across platforms (social media, websites, conferences).

4. **Keep It Authentic and Transparent**

   - **Bad storytelling:** Overly scripted, exaggerated claims, stock-photo patients.
   - **Great Storytelling:** Real people, raw emotions, genuine struggles, and triumphs.

   Example: GSK's "More Than Medicine" Campaign"

   Instead of just promoting their medications, GSK highlighted how their employees and research impact real people's lives.

How to do it:

- Be truthful — don't overpromise.
- Use real patient voices instead of paid actors when possible.
- Show the ups and downs of treatment journeys.

5. **Leverage Social Media and Digital Channels**

   Social media has changed storytelling — it is no longer just brands talking; it is a conversation.

   Example — #RAWarrior (Rheumatoid Arthritis Community)

   Instead of a pharma company broadcasting a one-sided message, they encouraged patients to share their RA journeys, creating a thriving community.

   How to do it:

   - Encourage user-generated content.
   - Create hashtags for patient communities.
   - Use live Q&As with doctors and patient advocates.

Final Thoughts: Storytelling is the Future of Pharma Marketing

People do not connect with products — they connect with stories.

- Make patients the heroes.
- Use emotions to drive engagement.
- Be authentic, transparent, and human.

Because, at the end of the day, pharma marketing is not just about selling treatments — It is about changing lives.

CHAPTER 7

Why Storytelling Matters in Pharma

Picture this: A doctor enters a conference, and two speakers take the stage. The first one jumps straight into clinical trial data, rattling off statistics and molecular mechanisms. The second one starts with a story about a real patient who struggled, found hope, and transformed their life thanks to a breakthrough treatment.

Which one do you think the audience will remember?

That's the power of storytelling.

In pharma, we deal with some of the most complex, life-changing, and emotionally charged topics — disease, hope, survival, and trust. Yet, for years, pharma marketing has leaned heavily on numbers, compliance-heavy messaging, and scientific jargon. But here is the thing:

People do not remember facts. They remember how something made them feel.

So, why does storytelling matter in pharma? Let's break it down.

1. **Stories Make Science Understandable**

   Let's be honest—pharmaceuticals are full of big words and complex data. While necessary, this information can overwhelm patients and healthcare professionals.

   A story makes it human. It translates science into something relatable, something a person can see themselves in.

Example: Instead of saying, "This drug reduces HbA1C by 1.2% in Type 2 Diabetes patients."

Tell the story of Anna, who struggled with her diabetes for years but finally got it under control and regained her energy thanks to this treatment.

Why it works: A real-life example makes the impact of the drug tangible.

2. **Stories Build Emotional Connections**

People do not connect with data — they connect with people.

Doctors, patients, and caregivers do not just want to know the efficacy rate of a medication. They want to understand:

- How will it change someone's life?
- Will this give hope to a struggling patient?
- Can this restore a father's ability to play with his kids?

Example: Pharma brands like Roche have used real patient stories in their cancer campaigns, showing how their treatments help people live fuller lives.

Why it works: Emotions drive decisions. When doctors see how a treatment helps a real patient, they are more likely to remember and trust it.

3. **Stories Build Trust in an Industry That Needs It**

Let's be real—the pharmaceutical industry has trust issues. Many people approach it with skepticism because they have concerns about drug pricing, safety, and ethics.

A well-told, authentic story can change perception faster than any corporate statement ever could.

Example: Instead of just saying, "We are committed to patient well-being,"

Pharmaceutical companies can share real stories of:

- Researchers working tirelessly to develop treatments.
- Doctors going the extra mile for patients.
- How a company supported a patient in need through an assistance program.

Why it works: Authenticity builds credibility. When people see the real faces behind pharma, they are more likely to trust the industry.

4. **Stories Influence Decision-Making**

   Science backs this up: Stories activate more areas of the brain than plain facts.

   When people hear data, only the brain's language center lights up.

   When people hear a story, it activates multiple senses, triggering empathy, memory, and even mirroring neurons, making them feel like they are experiencing the story themselves.

   This means:

   - Doctors are more likely to recall a treatment if they remember a patient's story tied to it.
   - Patients are more likely to trust a brand that tells a relatable story.
   - Caregivers are more likely to advocate for a treatment when they see how it has helped others.

   Example: Instead of saying. "This drug reduces seizures in epilepsy by 50%."

   Tell the story of a young boy who can now go to school without fear of a seizure disrupting his day.

   Why it works: Stories turn abstract concepts into personal experiences.

5. **Stories Help Differentiate Brands**

   Let's face it: Many drugs within the same therapeutic area have similar clinical profiles.

   So, what makes a doctor choose one brand over another?

   - A strong emotional connection.
   - A story that sticks in their mind.

   Example: Nike and Apple sell more than shoes and gadgets—they sell inspirational stories. Similarly, a pharmaceutical brand that tells a compelling narrative about how its treatment changes lives will stand out in a crowded market.

Why it works: Stories create loyalty. When people connect emotionally with a brand, they remember it.

6. **Stories Make Pharma More Human**

   Pharma is not just about drugs. It's about:

   - People.
   - Hope.
   - Saving lives.

   A brand that shares real, human stories — from patients, doctors, and researchers — becomes more than just a pharmaceutical company. It becomes a trusted healthcare partner.

   Example: Pfizer's COVID-19 vaccine campaign did not just discuss mRNA technology—it also shared the story of the scientists who worked day and night to make it happen.

   Why it works: People want to see the heart behind the science.

Final Thoughts: Storytelling is the Future of Pharma Marketing

If there is one thing to remember, it is this:

- Facts tell, but stories sell.
- Stories make science relatable.
- Stories create emotional bonds.
- Stories build trust.
- Stories drive decisions.
- Stories make brands memorable.

In a world where attention spans are shrinking, the brands that tell the best stories will be the ones that win.

Because, at the end of the day, pharma is not just about medicine — it's about changing lives. And nothing communicates that better than a great story.

Building Trust in A Regulated Industry

The Pharma Challenge

Let's be honest —pharma has a trust problem.

Patients often perceive the industry as profit-driven, healthcare professionals (HCPs) question the authenticity of marketing messages, and regulatory bodies monitor every word brands say. How can pharmaceutical companies build and maintain trust in a world where people are more skeptical than ever?

The answer? Authenticity, transparency, and — most importantly — storytelling.

But let's break it down step by step.

Why Trust is Hard to Earn in Pharma

Pharma operates in one of the most highly regulated industries. Every claim must be backed by clinical evidence, every marketing message must comply with strict regulations, and patient safety must always come first.

Yet despite these rules, trust in the industry has been shaken by:

- Drug pricing concerns — "Are medications too expensive?"
- Safety controversies — "Are side effects being downplayed?
- Misinformation — "What should I believe — the science of social media?"
- The opioid crisis, recalls, and past scandals — "Are pharma companies truly patient-centric?"

The bottom line is that people don't trust companies just because they say, "Trust us." Trust has to be earned over time.

How Can Pharma Build Trust?

1. **Be Transparent — No Fine Print Needed**

   Trust starts with openness. Pharma companies can't afford to sound secretive or overly corporate. Instead, they should be clear about"

   - How drugs are developed — The research process, safety trials, and real-world evidence.
   - Side effects and limitations — No sugarcoating. Acknowledge the risks.
   - Pricing and access programs — Show what is being done to make treatments accessible.

   Example: Novo Nordisk, a leader in diabetes care, openly discusses the cost of insulin and what they are doing to address affordability concerns. This type of transparency makes companies more relatable.

2. **Humanize the Brand — Tell Stories, Not Just Science**

   Science is important, but it alone won't win hearts. What makes pharmaceuticals relatable are the people behind the science and the patients who benefit from it.

   - Instead of just publishing clinical trial results, share a patient's journey.
   - Instead of just listing drug benefits, show a doctor explaining how it changed lives.
   - Instead of just talking about corporate social responsibility, spotlight the researchers who dedicate their lives to finding cures.

   Example: Gilead Sciences, in its HIV awareness campaigns, does not just talk about medicines — it shares real stories of individuals living with HIV and how they regained control of their lives.

3. **Engage with Healthcare Professionals Authentically**

   Doctors and healthcare professionals are at the frontlines of patient care. Pharma companies need to move beyond traditional sales pitches and engage HCPs in a way that builds long-term trust.

- Provide value through education. HCPs trust pharma companies that offer credible, data-driven, and practical insights.
- Be a partner, not a salesperson. Support HCPs with resources to help them make informed decisions rather than just pushing products.
- Listen. Instead of just talking to HCPs, engage them in a two-way discussion about their challenges and needs.

Example: Medtronic, a medical device company, builds trust by offering continuing medical education for HCPs. It focuses on improving patient care rather than just selling its products.

4. **Be Honest in Crisis Situations**

If something goes wrong — a drug recall, a safety concern, or negative press — don't hide. Own it.

- Acknowledge the issue — Don't delay or deflect.
- Take responsibility — Show what is being done to fix the problem.
- Communicate proactively — Keep patients, HCPs, and stakeholders informed.

Example: When Johnson & Johnson faced concerns over some of its products, it actively engaged with the public, addressed the issues, and reinforced safety measures. This approach prevented further damage to its reputation.

5. **Leverage Digital and Social Media Responsibly**

Today, trust is not just built in boardrooms — it is built online. Patients and HCPs turn to social media, forums, and digital content for medical information.

- Use social media to educate and engage. Don't just post ads — Share valuable insights.
- Combat misinformation proactively. If false claims about a drug spread online, address them with science-backed, easy-to-understand explanations.

- Showcase real voices. Patients, doctors, and researchers can be more persuasive than corporate spokespeople.

Example: Pfizer and Moderna used digital platforms to address COVID-19 vaccine hesitancy, providing clear, science-backed, yet approachable messaging.

6. **Focus on Long-Term Relationships, Not Just Transactions**

A brand that only appears when it is time to promote a new drug would not build lasting trust. Companies that establish consistent, meaningful engagement will stand out.

- Invest in patient communities — Support groups, disease awareness campaigns, and patient advocacy initiatives.
- Engage with policymakers and regulators — Be a part of the healthcare conversation, not just a bystander.
- Support ethical and sustainable practices — Commitment to patient welfare over profit wins credibility.

Example: Merck's long-term commitment to fighting river blindness in Africa through its Mectizan donation program has earned it lasting respect.

The Bottom Line: Trust is Earned, Not Given

Trust in pharma does not come from more ads, bigger budgets, or loud messaging. It comes from:

- Transparency — Say what you mean, mean what you say.
- Authenticity —Show the real people behind the science.
- Consistency — Trust is built over time, not in a single campaign.
- Empathy — Put patients first, always.

At its heart, pharmaceuticals are not just about making medicines—they're about saving and improving lives. Companies that understand this and communicate with honesty, compassion, and credibility will earn lasting trust.

Connecting with Patients, Physicians, and Stakeholders

Pharma marketing is not just about science and numbers—it is about people. Patients battle chronic illnesses, doctors make life-changing decisions, caregivers look for answers, and investors ensure the future of healthcare. To truly make an impact, pharmaceutical brands must connect with each of these audiences in a way that feels real, relevant, and human.

That's where storytelling comes in.

Great storytelling is not about selling a product but creating meaningful connections. Let's explore how pharma can use storytelling to build trust and engagement with three key audiences: patients, physicians, and stakeholders.

Connecting with Patients: Speak to Their Hearts: Not Just Their Conditions

When a patient receives a diagnosis, they don't just need a drug name and a list of side effects – they need hope, clarity, and reassurance. Patients want to know:

- "How will this treatment help me live a better life?"
- "What do others like me experience?"
- "Can I trust this company to have my best interests at heart?"

How Pharma Can Connect:

- Share patient stories. Seeing someone else's journey can help patients feel less alone.
- Use simple, empathetic language. Avoid medical jargon and explain things in a personal and relatable way.
- Empower patients with knowledge. Provide content that helps them make informed decisions about their health.

Example: Roche's breast cancer awareness campaigns go beyond clinical data. They feature real patients who share their emotional experiences from diagnosis to treatment, helping others feel seen and supported.

Connecting with Physicians: Be a Partner, Not Just a Pharma Rep

Doctors are busy. They must manage patient care, research, and stay current with medical advancements. The last thing they need is a sales pitch.

Physicians want to know:

- "How does this treatment improve patient outcomes?"
- "Is there solid clinical evidence to support it?"
- "What makes this therapy different from others available?"

How Pharma Can Connect:

- Be a trusted source of knowledge. Share insights from real-world evidence, clinical trials, and patient case studies.
- Provide tools that make their job easier. Decision-support tools, treatment guidelines, and digital resources can help HCPs make informed choices.
- Engage in meaningful conversations. Instead of a one-way information dump, create forums for peer discussions and expert collaborations.

Example: Medtronic does not just promote medical devices — it provides continuing education courses for doctors, ensuring they are partners in advancing healthcare.

Connecting with Stakeholders: Show the Bigger Picture

Pharma companies do not operate in a vacuum. Investors, regulators, payers, and policymakers influence how medicines reach patients. Winning their trust requires more than financial reports; it requires a compelling vision.

Stakeholders want to know:

- "What impact is this company making on healthcare?"

- "Is this brand committed to ethical and sustainable practices?"
- "How is this company shaping the future of medicine?"

How Pharma can connect:

- Share the "why" behind your work. What motivates your company beyond profits? How are you making a difference in global health?
- Highlight corporate responsibility. Showcase efforts in accessibility, patient advocacy, and environmental sustainability.
- Be transparent. Openly communicate about pricing, research investments, and ethical business practices.

Example: Gilead Sciences does not just report on profits; they highlight their commitment to curing diseases like Hepatitis C and making treatments accessible in low-income countries.

The Power of Connection: One Story, Many Audiences

The beauty of storytelling? A single story can connect with multiple audiences in different ways.

- A patient hears a story of someone like them and feels hopeful.
- A doctor sees a case study and gains confidence in a treatment.
- A stakeholder recognizes the brand's commitment to innovation.

At the core of it all, pharma is not just about drugs — it's about people. And when pharma brands use storytelling to connect on a human level, they move from corporations to be trusted partners in health.

Addressing Ethical and Compliance Challenges

Navigating the Tightrope

Storytelling in pharmaceutical marketing is not just about crafting compelling narratives—it's about doing so ethically and responsibly. Unlike other industries, where marketers can take creative liberties, pharmaceuticals operate under strict regulations to ensure that patient safety, transparency, and scientific accuracy are never compromised.

So, how do you tell an engaging, persuasive story while staying compliant? It's a delicate balance — but one that is entirely possible when done right.

Why Ethical and Compliant Storytelling Matters

Imagine a pharmaceutical company running a heartfelt campaign featuring a patient whose life was changed by a breakthrough drug. The story is powerful, but what if the claims overpromise results or omit risks? Suddenly, what was meant to inspire becomes misleading and legally problematic.

What is at stake?

- Loss of trust — Patients and HCPs need accurate, balanced information.
- Legal penalties — Regulatory bodies like the FDA, EMA, and other agencies enforce strict guidelines.
- Brand reputation damage — A single misleading claim can trigger a public backlash.

In short, if your storytelling is not ethical, it is not effective.

The Key Compliance Challenges in Pharma Storytelling

So, what are the biggest compliance pitfalls in pharma marketing? Here are a few key areas to watch out for:

- Misleading Claims and Overpromising
  - Don't use vague, exaggerated, or emotionally charged language that implies guaranteed success (e.g., "This drug will change your life forever!).
  - Do stick to evidence-based claims and clinical trial data. Use language that is hopeful yet responsible.
- Balancing Emotion with Scientific Accuracy
  - Don't let the emotional power of the patient's story override medical facts (e.g., highlighting a rare, miraculous recovery as if it is the norm).
  - Complement personal stories with real-world data and disclaimers to provide a complete picture.
- Fair Balance: Risks vs. Benefits
  - Don't highlight only the positives while downplaying potential side effects.
  - Provide a clear, honest discussion of risks and benefits to empower informed decision-making.
- Patient Privacy and Consent
  - Don't use patient testimonials or case studies without explicit informed consent.
  - Ensure all HIPAA (or GDPR) guidelines are followed, and anonymize patient data if needed.
- Respecting Regulations on Off-Label Promotion
  - Don't suggest a drug can treat conditions outside its approved indications.
  - Stick to the approved indications and communicate within regulatory frameworks.

How to Tell Powerful Yet Ethical Stories

So, how can pharma marketers create authentic, engaging stories while staying compliant? Here is a practical approach:

1. **Be Transparent and Honest**
   - If your product has risks, acknowledge them.

- If a treatment works only for certain patients, say so.
- If there are alternative therapies, mention them.

Example: Instead of claiming "95% of patients recover in weeks," say:

"In a clinical study, 95% of participants experienced improvement within 'X' weeks. Individual results may vary."

2. **Make Compliance a Creative Challenge, Not a Roadblock**

   Many marketers see compliance as an obstacle to creativity, but it can be an opportunity to build trust and credibility.

   - Instead of making exaggerated claims, use real patient journeys with factual outcomes.
   - Instead of sensationalized visuals, use storytelling techniques that highlight empathy and data side by side.
   - Instead of avoiding risk discussions, frame them as part of the informed decision-making process.

   Example: Novo Nordisk's diabetes campaigns use real patient voices while ensuring all medical claims are backed by scientific evidence.

3. **Use Disclaimers Smartly Without Killing the Story**

   Let's face it — nobody enjoys reading the fine print. But in pharma, disclaimers are essential. The trick? Integrate them seamlessly into your storytelling.

   - Instead of: A block of dense text at the bottom
   - Try breaking disclaimers into digestible, easy-to-read statements within the narrative.

   Example: If featuring a patient success story, a simple note like "Individual experiences may vary. Consult your physician to see if this treatment is right for you" maintains transparency without disrupting engagement.

The Future: AI and Ethical Storytelling

New ethical challenges are emerging with AI and generative content tools becoming part of pharma marketing.

AI-powered stories must be:

- Fact-checked against medical literature
- Reviewed for bias and misinformation
- Transparent about AI involvement in content creation

Companies embracing ethical AI storytelling will gain a competitive edge by ensuring their narratives remain credible, compliant, and consumer-friendly.

Final Thoughts: Storytelling with Integrity

Ethical storytelling is about building trust. Patients, physicians, and regulators all want the same thing: truthful, transparent, and meaningful communication.

When done right, pharma storytelling can:

- Inspire hope while staying honest
- Educate while staying compliant
- Engage without misleading

And most importantly? It can build a legacy of trust that lasts far beyond a single campaign.

CHAPTER

8

How to Craft an Effective Pharma Story

Crafting an Effective Pharma Story: The Perfect Blend of Science and Emotion

Storytelling in pharmaceutical marketing is not just about narrating a patient's journey or showcasing a breakthrough drug — it's about connecting, educating, and inspiring action while remaining credible and compliant.

So, how do you craft a story that engages hearts, satisfies regulators, and drives decisions? Let's break it down.

1. **Step 1: Define Your Core Message**

   Before you start weaving words, ask yourself:

   - What's the one thing my audience should take away?
     - Is it hope? Awareness? Understanding? A call to action?
     - **Example**: "Diabetes management is more than medication — it is a journey of small victories."
   - Who is this story for?
     - Patients? Doctors? Caregivers? Investors?
     - **Example**: A patient's story might focus on emotional transformation, while a doctor's story might emphasize clinical outcomes.
   - What action do I want them to take?

- Talk to their doctor? Try a new treatment? Sign up for a support program?
- **Example**: "By recognizing the early signs, you can take control of your health today."

A great pharma story is crisp, focused, and purposeful.

2. **Step 2: Start with a Human-Centric Hook**

   People connect with people, not products. That's why your story should start with a real-world moment.

   Instead of:

   "Our medication is backed by groundbreaking research."

   Try:

   "For years, Emily struggled with migraines so severe they stole her days and disrupted her life. Then she found a treatment that gave her freedom back."

   Why? Because humans resonate with humans. We see ourselves in their struggles and triumphs.

3. **Step 3: Use the Classic Story Arc**

   The best pharma stories follow a structure that makes them relatable, engaging, and easy to remember.

   1. **The Challenge (the 'Before')**
      - Introduce the problem — pain, fear, frustration
      - Make it personal and vivid
      - **Example**: "When James was diagnosed with rheumatoid arthritis, everyday tasks — tying his shoes, holding a cup of coffee cup — became painful battles."
   2. **The Turning Point (Discovery and Solution)**
      - Introduce the product, therapy, or breakthrough
      - Show how it works without overselling
      - **Example**: "His doctor introduced him to a new treatment that helped manage inflammation, restoring movement he thought he had lost forever."

3. **The Resolution (The 'After')**
    - Show life post-solution — what has improved?
    - Make it realistic — (no 'miracle cures')
    - **Example:** "Today, James enjoys morning walks again, pain-free."

Remember: Even when telling a product-related story, focus on the human transformation, not just the drug.

4. **Step 4: Keep it Simple and Jargon-Free**

   Pharma marketing is tricky because it involves complex science. However, effective storytelling means translating that science into everyday language.

   Instead of:

   "Our monoclonal antibody therapy inhibits TNF-alpha to modulate the inflammatory response."

   Try:

   "This treatment helps calm inflammation, making daily activities easier and less painful.

   The simpler and clearer your story, the more people will connect with it.

5. **Step 5: Use Emotion — But Stay Ethical**

   Emotion makes stories memorable, but in pharma, it has to be used responsibly.

   - Do
     - Highlight real struggles and triumphs
     - Balance emotion with science
     - Provide honest outcomes
   - Don't
     - Use exaggerated or misleading claims
     - Overpromise results
     - Downplay risks

- **Example:**
  - Ethical: "Most patients see improvements within a few weeks, but results vary."
  - Misleading: "You will feel better instantly — guaranteed!"

A strong story is emotional, yet factual.

6. **Step 6: Include a Clear Call to Action (CTA)**

   A great story inspires action. But what do you want the audience to do next?

   - For patients: "Talk to your doctor today to see if this treatment is right for you."
   - For doctors: "Join our online community for support and resources."

   Your CTA should be a natural next step in the story, not a sales pitch.

7. **Step 7: Choose the Right Format and Platform**

   Not all stories fit all formats. Tailor yours to where your audience is.

   - Videos and Animations — Great for emotional impact (e.g., patient journeys)
   - Infographics — Ideal for breaking down complex science.
   - Blog Posts and Articles — Best for educational deep dives.
   - Social Media — Perfect for short, snackable storytelling moments.
   - **Example**: AstraZeneca's patient videos for lung cancer treatment use real people, not actors, sharing their experiences in a documentary-style format, creating authentic, emotional engagement.

Final Thoughts: Stories That Stick

A well-crafted pharma story is:

- Human-centered — Focus on people, not just products.

- Structured — Every great story has a beginning, middle, and end.
- Simple and Clear — No unnecessary medical jargon.
- Emotional yet Ethical — Inspire trust, not false hope.
- Actionable — A great story should lead to the next step.

When done right, storytelling is not just a marketing tool but a bridge connecting science with the human experience. In pharmaceuticals, that connection can change lives.

Elements of A Compelling Story: Characters, Conflict, and Resolution

Every great story—whether it is a bestselling novel, a blockbuster movie, or a powerful pharma marketing campaign—relies on three essential elements: characters, conflict, and resolution.

Without characters, there is no one to root for.

Without conflict, there is nothing to keep us engaged.

Without resolution, we are left without closure.

Let us explore these elements and see how they come to life in pharma storytelling.

1. **Characters: The Heart of Your Story**

   At the core of every compelling story is someone we care about. It's the character that draws us in, makes us feel, and keeps us invested in the journey.

   - In pharmaceutical marketing, your characters could be:
   - Patients—Experiencing a challenge or transformation.
   - Doctors—Navigating treatment options for better patient outcomes.
   - Caregivers—Supporting loved ones through their health journeys.
   - Scientists and Researchers—Pushing the boundaries of medical innovation.

   Example: Instead of saying "Our drug treats rheumatoid arthritis," introduce us to Lisa, a mother of two, struggling with joint pain that makes it difficult to hold her child's hand.

   Why It Works: People connect with people, not products. A real, relatable character makes the story feel personal and meaningful.

How to Create Relatable Characters:

- Give them names, emotions, and relatable struggles.
- Make them authentic—no exaggerated or unrealistic personas.
- Keep it realistic and hopeful—audiences relate to both challenges and triumphs.

2. **Conflict: The Challenge That Drives Engagement**

Conflict is what makes a story interesting. It's the struggle, challenge, or obstacle that keeps us invested in what happens next.

In pharma storytelling, the conflict often revolves around:

- The burden of disease—How it affects everyday life.
  - The uncertainty of treatment options—Finding the right solution.
  - Emotional and psychological struggles—Fear, frustration, or hope.

Example: Instead of "Our treatment improves quality of life," say:

"After years of struggling with insomnia, Alex felt like a prisoner of his own exhaustion. No medication seemed to work— until his doctor introduced him to a new therapy."

Why it works: Conflict creates tension and makes us care about the outcome.

How to Craft an Engaging Conflict:

- Keep it realistic and relatable.
- Show the impact on daily life.
- Don't overdramatize—balance authenticity with hope.

3. **Resolution: The Satisfying Conclusion**

Resolution brings the story full circle. It's the solution, a breakthrough, or a transformation that provides closure.

In pharma marketing, this could be:

- A treatment that improves quality of life.
- A support program that helps patients cope,
- A doctor discovering a breakthrough solution.

Example: Instead of saying, "Our therapy is effective," conclude with:

"Today, Alex wakes up refreshed, something he had not experienced in years. He is finally reclaiming his energy and joy."

Why it works: A strong resolution gives hope, shows progress, and reinforces the impact of your solution.

How to Create a Meaningful Resolution:

- Focus on the transformation (not just the product).
- Keep it realistic— no "miracle cures."
- End with a call to action—What should the audience do next?

Bringing it All Together: A Mini Pharma Story

Before: "Our drug treats severe asthma and helps patients breathe easier."

After (with storytelling)

"For years, Mia felt like a prisoner to her asthma. Even a short walk left her gasping for air, forcing her to sit out on family hikes and adventures. No treatment seemed to work. Then her doctor introduced her to a new therapy designed for people like her. Now, for the first time in years, she can run with her kids at the park—without fear."

See the difference? The second version:

- Introduces a character we can relate to.
- Shows a conflict that builds engagement.
- Ends with a resolution that gives hope.

Final Thoughts: Why This Matters in Pharma

Effective storytelling is not just about selling a product—it's about building connections, trust, and understanding.

- Characters make stories personal.
- Conflict keeps audiences engaged.
- Resolution provides hope and drives action.

When done right, storytelling transforms pharma marketing from clinical messaging into something deeply human and emotionally powerful.

Aligning Stories with Brand Purpose and Values

The Heartbeat of Pharma Storytelling

Imagine you walk into a bookstore looking for a good read. You pick up a book with a stunning cover, an intriguing title, and a promising blurb. But as you start reading, the story does not make sense. The characters lack depth, the plot jumps around, and by the time you reach the middle, you are lost. You close the book and move on.

Now, consider this in the context of pharma marketing: If a brand tells stories that feel disconnected from its core purpose and values, people, whether patients, physicians, or stakeholders, will lose interest and, worse, they will lose trust.

That is why aligning storytelling with brand purpose and values is critical. Your audience is not just looking for information; they are looking for authenticity, credibility, and emotional connection. Let us explore how to achieve that.

Step 1: Know Your Brand's "Why"

Every great story has a core message—something it tries to communicate more deeply. For pharma brands, this message should be rooted in your purpose:

- Why do we exist beyond selling medicine?
- What impact do we want to have on people's lives?
- How do we define success beyond revenue?

Example: If your company is built around the idea of helping people with chronic conditions live better lives, then your stories should focus on empowerment, resilience, and patient journeys, not just clinical efficacy.

Step 2: Identify Your Core Values and Make Them Visible

Your brand's values should be more than words in a mission statement—they should shine through in every story you tell. Ask yourself:

- Are we emphasizing compassion in our patient stories?
- Are we showcasing trust and transparency in how we present data?
- Are we highlighting innovation through breakthrough discoveries?

Example: If your brand stands for patient-centricity, don't just create ads about your product. Instead, share real stories of how your solutions have transformed lives—how a mother regained energy to play with her kids, or how a patient returned to their passion for running after treatment.

Step 3: Craft Stories That Bring Your Purpose to Life

Now, let us bring everything together. Your brand's purpose and values should shape the types of stories you tell:

- Patient Success Stories—Show real-life impact in an empathetic and inspiring way.
- Physician Narratives—Highlight how healthcare professionals trust your brand to improve patient care.
- Behind-the-Scenes Stories—Showcase your scientists, researchers, and employees driven by the brand's mission.

Example: Instead of saying, "Our drug improves survival rates," tell a story about a patient who saw their daughter graduate because of your treatment. Instead of saying, "We prioritize innovation," show how your researchers worked tirelessly for a decade to develop a breakthrough therapy.

Step 4: Keep It Consistent Across All Channels

A brand story is not just one campaign—It's the sum of everything you put into the world. Every touchpoint should reinforce your message:

- Website and Social Media—Are we telling stories that reflect our mission?
- Marketing and Sales Materials—Do these highlight our values authentically?
- Internal Culture—Do our employees believe in and live by these values?

Example: If your brand stands for trust and transparency, don't just preach it—practice it by sharing clear, honest information with physicians and patients, even if it means acknowledging challenges.

Final Thought: Stories That Stay With People

At the end of the day, stories stick when they feel real, meaningful, and aligned with a brand's values. Pharma marketing is about more than just science—it's about human lives, hope, and impact. When your stories reflect your purpose and values, they don't just inform; they inspire, connect, and build trust.

So, what's the story your brand is telling? And more importantly, does it feel true to who you are?

Adapting Stories for Different Audiences

Speaking Their Language, Winning Their Hearts

Imagine you are telling a bedtime story to a child. You would not use complex medical jargon or industry buzzwords, right? Now, imagine explaining the same story to a group of scientists. You would tweak the details, add more depth, and use precise language. The core story remains the same, but how you tell it changes depending on the audience.

This is exactly how storytelling in pharma marketing should work. A great story is not just about what you say—It is about how you say it to the right people. Whether you are engaging patients, physicians, payers, or policymakers, adapting your storytelling approach is key to making a lasting impact.

Let us break it down.

Step 1: Know Your Audience's Mindset

Each group has different concerns, priorities, and levels of knowledge. Understanding what matters to them helps shape the tone, language, and focus of your story.

A. Physicians and Healthcare Professionals

- *What they care about*: Clinical evidence, patient outcomes, new treatment options.
- *How to engage them*: Use data-driven narratives, patient case studies, and real-world clinical experiences.

- **Example**: Instead of saying, "Our drug changes lives," say, "In a recent study, 85% of patients reported significant pain relief within two weeks."

B. Patients and Caregivers

- *What they care about*: Quality of life, emotional impact, hope, and empowerment.

- *How to engage them*: Use empathy-driven storytelling, personal experiences, and relatable language.
- **Example**: Instead of focusing on statistics, share a patient's journey: "After years of struggling with symptoms, Sarah finally found a treatment that lets her enjoy life again."

C. Payers and Policymakers

- *What they care about*: Cost-effectiveness, long-term value, healthcare impact.
- *How to engage them*: Use economic storytelling, healthcare system insights, and big picture thinking.
- **Example**: "By reducing hospitalizations by 30%, this treatment saves the healthcare system millions annually."

D. Internal Teams and Sales Reps

- *What they care about*: Brand vision, product differentiation, storytelling techniques.
- *How to engage them*: Provide memorable brand stories, clear product positioning, and storytelling training.
- **Example**: Instead of listing product benefits, equip them with real-world success stories they can share.

Step 2: Adjust the Tone, Language, and Format

Once you know your audience, tweak your storytelling approach to match their expectations.

A. For Physicians — Professional, precise, scientific

- Use case studies, medical imagery, and peer-reviewed data.
- **Example**: A video featuring a respected doctor explaining the mechanism of action.

B. For Patients—Emotional, Relatable, Easy to understand

- Use real patient stories, simple visuals, and clear language.
- **Example**: A heartfelt testimonial video of a patient sharing their journey.

C. For Payers—Strategic, high-level, data-backed

- Use health economics data, cost-benefit analysis, and long-term projections.

- **Example**: An infographic comparing treatment costs and outcomes.

Step 3: Choose the Right Channel

Even the most compelling story will fall flat if delivered on the wrong platform. Tailor your distribution strategy based on where your audience is most engaged.

- *Physicians*: Medical journals, conferences, webinars, LinkedIn
- *Patients*: Social media, patient advocacy groups, YouTube, websites
- *Payers*: Policy briefings, whitepapers, executive presentations
- *Sales Teams*: Training workshops, storytelling guides, interactive tools

Final Thoughts: One Story, Many Voices

The key to adapting pharmaceutical storytelling is not changing the message but reshaping the delivery to resonate with each audience. Whether you are talking to a doctor, a patient, or a healthcare policymaker, your story should meet them where they are and speak to what matters most to them.

So, next time you craft a story, ask yourself: Who is listening? How can I make it truly meaningful to them?

CHAPTER

9

The Storytelling Framework

Crafting Stories That Stick

Think about the last time a story truly captivated you—one that stayed long after you heard it. Maybe a patient's journey, a breakthrough discovery, or a brand's mission resonated deeply. What made it unforgettable? It had structure.

Great stories don't just happen—they follow a framework. And in pharma marketing, where trust, credibility, and emotional connection matter, structuring your story the right way makes all the difference.

Let's break down a powerful storytelling framework that ensures your message is heard, felt, and remembered.

Step 1: The Hook—Grabbing Attention Instantly

People decide within seconds whether they will engage with your story. So, start strong. The hook should instantly spark curiosity, emotion, or urgency.

- *For patients*: "Imagine living with constant pain—until one day, everything changes."
- *For physicians*: "What if you could reduce patient hospitalizations by 30%—without changing your treatment protocol?"

- *For Payers*: "Every year, ineffective treatments cost healthcare systems billions. But what if there was a better way?"

The key? Make it relevant, intriguing, and personal.

Step 2: The Challenge—Defining the Problem

Every great story has conflict—a problem that needs solving. In pharma, this could be:

- A medical condition that patients struggle with
- A treatment gap that physicians face
- A financial burden for healthcare systems

Your audience should see themselves in the problem.

- *For patients*: "Lisa was a young mother who loved running—until rheumatoid arthritis made even walking painful."
- *For physicians*: "Doctors face a tough choice: prescribe a treatment with serious side effects or leave symptoms unmanaged."
- *For Payers*: "Despite new therapies, adherence remains low, leading to costly hospital readmissions."

Once the problem is clear, the audience is invested in finding a solution.

Step 3: The Journey—Introducing the Solution

Now, it's time to bring in your brand, product, or idea—but in a way that feels natural, not salesy.

The best way? Show Transformation.

- How does the treatment work?
- How does it impact real lives?
- What makes it different?

- *For patients*: "Then Lisa's doctor introduced her to a new treatment—one that did not just manage symptoms but gave her back her life."
- *For physicians*: "A breakthrough therapy is changing the way we approach this disease, improving both efficacy and patient adherence."
- *For payers*: "With a single intervention, healthcare systems can reduce costs while improving patient outcomes."

Instead of listing features, demonstrate impact.

Step 4: The Resolution—The Emotional Payoff

People remember how a story makes them feel. End with a strong resolution that leaves an impression.

- Did a patient regain their quality of life?
- Did a physician find a better way to treat their patients?
- Did a healthcare system save money while improving care?
- *For Patients*: "Today, Lisa is back to running marathons, thanks to a treatment that truly works for her."
- *For physicians*: "Now doctors have a treatment option that aligns with their clinical expertise and patient needs."
- *For payers*: "This solution is not just innovative— it is a smart, sustainable investment for healthcare."

The goal? Leave your audience feeling inspired, reassured, or excited about what is possible.

Final Thought: Make Every Story Count

A compelling pharmaceutical story follows a clear structure:

- *Hook*: Grab attention
- *Challenge*: Define the problem

- *Journey*: Present the Solution
- *Resolution*: Deliver the emotional payoff

Whether you are talking to patients, doctors, or decision-makers, the framework remains the same—only the details change.

So, the next time you craft a story, ask yourself: Am I just informing, or am I truly engaging? If you follow this framework, your story won't just be heard—it will be remembered.

Step 1: Identifying Your Audience and Goals

Imagine walking into a room full of people and delivering a speech without knowing who they are, what they care about, or why they are even listening. Chances are, your words won't land the way you want them to.

That's why step one in storytelling—especially in pharma marketing— is knowing exactly who you are talking to and what you want to achieve.

Let's break it down.

Who Are You Speaking To? (Know Your Audience)

Not all pharma stories are meant for the same people. A powerful message for a patient might sound completely irrelevant to a physician, and a compelling pitch for a payer might leave a sales rep uninspired.

So, before you even start crafting your story, ask yourself:

- Who am I talking to? (Patients? Physicians? Payers? Internal teams?)
- What do they care about? (Health? Outcomes? Costs? Scientific credibility?)
- What are their biggest frustrations? (Side effects? Lack of time? Regulatory pressures?)
- How do they consume information? (Videos? Social media? Whitepapers? Face-to-Face discussions?)

By defining your audience clearly, you ensure your story resonates with their emotions, needs, and daily challenges.

Example: A physician-focused story should be backed by clinical evidence and real-world data.

A patient-focused story should emphasize empathy, hope, and real-life transformation.

A payer-focused story should highlight cost-effectiveness and long-term impact.

The more tailored your story, the stronger the connection.

What's Your Goal? (Define Your Purpose)

Every great story has a purpose—It's not just about telling an interesting tale, but about driving action.

So, before crafting your pharma story, ask yourself:

- What do I want my audience to think, feel, or do after hearing this story?
- Is my goal to educate, persuade, inspire, or build trust?
- What key message should they walk away with?

Different goals require different storytelling approaches.

- If your goal is education (e.g., raising disease awareness), focus on facts, patient journeys, and expert insights.
- If your goal is persuasion (e.g., getting a doctor to consider a new treatment), highlight scientific breakthroughs and patient success stories.
- If your goal is trust-building, center your story around transparency, ethics, and real-world impact.

Final Thought: Set the Stage for Success

If you skip this step, you risk crafting an ineffective story. Even a well-written story will not be effective if it does not speak to the right people in the right way.

So, before you start writing, take a moment to define:

- Who you are speaking to
- What they care about
- What action or change do you want to inspire

With these in place, you are not just telling a story—you are telling the right story to the right people in the right way.

Step 2: Unearthing Authentic Brand Stories

Have you ever sat through a generic corporate presentation that felt like it was crafted by a robot, full of jargon, statistics, and zero emotion? Compare that to a story that made you feel something—a patient's journey, a doctor's moment of realization, or a breakthrough that changed lives.

That's the power of authentic storytelling—it does not feel like marketing, it feels real.

But here is the challenge. How do you find these authentic brand stories?

Let's dig in.

Start with Real People, Not Just Data.

Your brand's most powerful stories don't come from the marketing department; they come from patients, healthcare professionals, researchers, and even your own employees.

Instead of crafting a story from thin air, go out and listen:

- Talk to patients. What was life like before and after treatment? What challenges did they overcome?
- Interview doctors. What was their "aha" moment when they decided to prescribe your therapy?
- Look inside your company. Is there an inspiring backstory about how a drug was developed? A researcher who would not give up?
- Review customer interactions. What are the common pain points, and how has your brand helped?

Your best stories are already happening— You just need to uncover them.

Find the Human Emotion in Your Brand's Journey

An authentic brand story is not just about facts; It's about the emotional journey behind those facts.

Ask yourself:

- What was the struggle? Every great story has a conflict—what challenges did patients, doctors, or researchers face?
- What was the turning point? Was there a breakthrough moment when everything changed?
- What was the impact? How did your brand make a real difference in someone's life?

Example: Instead of saying, "Our medication reduces HbA1C levels in Type 2 Diabetes patients,"

Tell the story of Sarah, a 42-year-old mom, who struggled with diabetes for years—until she found a treatment that gave her back control of her life.

See the difference? Facts inform, but stories inspire.

Keep It Real—No Overhyped Marketing Speak

In pharma, trust is everything. Patients, doctors, and payers are skeptical of stories that sound too good to be true.

So, when telling your brand's story:

- Avoid exaggerated claims ("This drug will change your life instantly!)
- Don't make the brand the hero (Our innovation saved the day!)
- Make the patient or doctor the hero. Your brand is just the guide that helped them succeed.

Example: Instead of "Our company's groundbreaking research led to a breakthrough in oncology,"

Say, "For years, Dr. Patel watched patients run out of options. Then, a new treatment emerged, giving them hope where there was none before."

Final Thought: Your Best Stories Are Already There—Go Find Them

The key to unearthing authentic brand stories is not creating them—It's discovering them.

- Listen to real experiences.
- Find the emotional core.
- Tell stories that feel genuine, not sales-driven.

Once you do, your storytelling will be effective, powerful, memorable, and deeply human.

Step 3: Designing A Multi-Channel Narrative

So, you have uncovered an authentic, compelling brand story. Great! But now comes a crucial question:

Where and how do you tell it?

Your audience—patients, physicians, or other stakeholders—is scattered across multiple platforms. They don't all engage with content in the same way. Some prefer videos, others social media, and some still read in-depth articles or whitepapers.

That's why a multi-channel narrative is key. It ensures your story reaches the right people in the right places, without feeling repetitive or disconnected.

Let's break it down.

One Story, Multiple Formats

Think of your story as a blockbuster movie. It doesn't just exist in theaters—it has trailers, behind-the-scenes interviews, social media clips, a novelization, and even a podcast discussing its impact.

Your brand story should work in the same way: one story, many formats.

- *Video*: A short emotional patient story for YouTube and social media.
- *Social Media Snippets*: Bite-sized versions of the story tailored for LinkedIn, Twitter (X now), and Instagram.
- *Articles and Blog Posts*: A deeper dive for medical professionals or industry insiders.
- *Infographics*: Key takeaways in a visually engaging format.
- *Webinars and Podcasts*: Extended discussions where experts can elaborate on the story's significance.

Example: Suppose your pharma brand has an incredible patient success story.

- The full journey could be shared in a 5-minute documentary video.
- Shorter 15-second clips could be posted on LinkedIn or Instagram.
- A detailed case study could appear on your website.
- A podcast episode could feature a doctor discussing the science behind the success.

One Story, many touchpoints.

Tailoring the Story for Different Audiences

Not everyone needs to hear the same version of the story. Doctors, patients, and investors all have different interests.

- **For Patients**:
  - Focus on emotion and impact—how the treatment changed a life.
  - Use simple, relatable language (avoid medical jargon).
  - Share stories on social media, YouTube, and patient communities.
- **For Physicians:**
  - Emphasize the scientific credibility and clinical outcomes.
  - Provide data, but through a compelling narrative.
  - Use webinars, medical conferences, and LinkedIn articles.
- **For Investors and Industry Insiders**:
  - Highlight the bigger picture—how your innovation is driving change.

- Frame the story around market impact and long-term vision.
- Use reports, case studies, and industry presentations.

Example: If your story is about a groundbreaking new cancer therapy,

- A patient version may highlight a survivor's emotional journey.
- A physician's version may focus on how the drug improved survival rates.
- An investor version may frame it as a disruptive innovation in oncology.

Same story, different angles.

Maintaining Consistency Across Channels

A multi-channel narrative does not mean telling completely different stories everywhere.

It means adapting the same core story while keeping a unified brand voice and message.

- Don't let the story get distorted or feel inconsistent across platforms.
- Ensure that every version aligns with your brand's values and key messages.

Think of your story as a music theme—it may sound different when played on a piano, a guitar, or a violin, but it's still the same melody.

Final Thought: Make Your Story Impossible to Miss

Designing a multi-channel narrative ensures your story reaches people wherever they are, without losing its power and authenticity.

- Repurpose your story into different formats.

- Adapt it for different audiences.
- Keep it consistent across all platforms.

When done right, your pharmaceutical brand's story will not only be told but also experienced, remembered, and shared.

Step 4: Refining and Testing Stories

Making Sure It Resonates

You have crafted a compelling pharma story, adapted it for different audiences, and planned how to distribute it across multiple channels. But here's the real test:

Does it actually connect with people?

A great story is not just something you tell and hope for the best. You refine, test, and optimize it based on how your audience reacts.

Let's explore how you ensure your story hits the right notes before launching it full-scale.

The Power of Refinement: Storytelling is a Process

Even the best stories don't nail it on the first try. Every great book, movie, or speech goes through multiple rounds of edits, feedback, and testing before it reaches its final form.

Your pharma brand story should be no different.

Here's how to refine your story:

- *Read it aloud*: Does it sound natural? Does it flow well?
- *Remove unnecessary complexity*: Are there parts that feel too technical or confusing?
- *Strengthen emotional impact*: Does the story evoke feelings? Does it inspire, build trust, or drive action?
- *Check for clarity and compliance*: Is the message clear, ethical, and aligned with regulatory guidelines?

Example: Suppose you are telling the story of a breakthrough treatment. If your first draft is full of dense medical jargon, your audience might lose interest. Refining it means simplifying the language without losing credibility.

Testing Your Story: Real Feedback from Real People

Once your story feels solid, it's time for a test run. You don't want to wait until the full launch to realize something is not working.

- **Small Focus Groups**
  - Gather a group of patients, physicians, or internal stakeholders and share the story.
  - Observe their reactions—do they seem engaged, confused, or indifferent?
  - Ask questions like: What stood out to you? Did anything feel unclear or unconvincing?
- **A/B Testing on Digital Platforms**
  - Try two slightly different versions of the story on a small scale (e.g., different headlines, tones, or story formats).
  - Track engagement: Which version gets more shares, likes, comments, or reading time?
  - Refine based on real-world audience behavior.
- **Social Media Pulse Check**
  - Post snippets of the story and monitor how people respond.
  - Did they engage? Do they ask follow-up questions?
  - If a certain phrase or message sparks more interest, emphasize that in the final version.
- **Internal Alignment**
  - Share your story with your internal teams—sales reps, medical affairs, and compliance experts.
  - Ensure everyone is comfortable and aligned with the messaging before it goes public.

Example: A pharmaceutical company launching a new diabetes awareness campaign could test two patient stories—one emphasizing lifestyle changes and another focusing on medical advancements. The one that gets the strongest response can be refined and scaled up.

Iteration: Keep Improving Your Story Over Time

A great story is not static—it evolves. You should continuously tweak and refine your storytelling approach based on feedback and real-world results.

- Monitor engagement metrics: What's working well? What's falling flat?
- Listen to your audience: Are patients or HCPs responding positively, or is there confusion?
- Adapt for future use: A story that works well in one market or platform may need to be adjusted for another.

Final Thought: The Best Stories Are the Ones That Connect

Storytelling in pharma is not just about what you say—it's about how well your audience receives it.

- Refine for clarity and emotional impact.
- Test with real audiences before a full rollout.
- Continuously optimize based on feedback.

When you refine and test your story, it does not just exist—it resonates, engages, and inspires action.

Step 5: Measuring Impact

Is Your Story Making A Difference

So, you have crafted an engaging pharma story, refined it based on feedback, and launched it across different channels. But here's the million-dollar question: Did it work?

Storytelling is not just about creativity—it's about impact. A great story should inspire action, change perceptions, and build connections. But you won't know if it's working unless you measure its effectiveness.

Let's discuss how you can track the success of your pharmaceutical storytelling and ensure it is driving the right results.

What Does Success Look Like?

Before diving into metrics, define what success means for your story. Are you aiming to:

- Build trust with patients and healthcare providers?
- Increase engagement on digital platforms?
- Improve brand recall and reputation?
- Drive a specific action, like patient inquiries or doctor recommendations?

Different goals require different measurement approaches.

For example:

- If you are launching a disease awareness campaign, success might mean more patient engagement and website visits.
- If you are telling a brand story, success might be increased trust and preference among physicians.
- If you are rolling out an internal storytelling initiative, success might mean better employee alignment with company values.

Once your goals are clear, you can measure the right things.

Key Metrics to Track Storytelling Impact

- Engagement Metrics (Are people paying attention?)
  - *Time spent on content*: Are people reading/watching your story till the end?
  - *Social media interactions*: Likes, shares, comments—do people feel compelled to engage?
  - *Video completion rates*: Are they watching the full patient story or skipping halfway?
- **Emotional and Sentiment Analysis (How do people feel about it?)**
  - *Social Listening*: Are patients and doctors talking about your story online?
  - *Survey & feedback forms*: Do people find your story relatable and inspiring?
  - *Brand sentiment tracking*: Has trust and perception of your brand improved?
- **Conversion Metrics (Is it driving action?)**
  - *Click-through rates (CTR)*: Are people taking the next step after seeing your story?
  - *Patient inquiries or doctor engagements*: Is the story leading to more interest in your product/service?
  - *Sales & prescription trends*: Are physicians more willing to recommend your treatment?
- **Internal Impact Metrics (Is your team aligned?)**
  - *Employee feedback*: Do sales reps and medical teams feel more connected to the brand story?
  - *Training engagement*: Are internal storytelling materials being used effectively?

Real-World Example: How Pharma Brands Measure Storytelling Impact

Imagine a pharmaceutical company launches a patient story campaign for a new migraine treatment.

- Before the campaign, they had low engagement with their educational materials.
  - After launching real patient stories, they measure:
  - 3x increase in time spent on content
  - 200% rise in social media shares
  - More HCPs requesting product information
  - A shift in brand sentiment, with more trust from patients

These insights help them fine-tune their next campaign and ensure storytelling continues to drive meaningful impact.

Refining Your Story Based on Results

Measuring impact is not just about collecting data—it's about learning and improving.

- If engagement is low, adjust the format (e.g., turn a long video into bite-sized clips).
- If trust is not increasing, highlight different patient perspectives or simplify the message.
- If doctors are not engaging, add more clinical validation or peer testimonials.

Great storytelling is not static—it evolves based on real-world impact.

Final Thought: The Best Stories Drive Action

Pharma storytelling is not just about telling—it's about connecting, engaging, and influencing. By measuring its impact, you ensure that your story is not just heard but makes a real difference.

So, what's next? Keep refining, keep optimizing, and keep telling stories that matter.

Part IV. Real-World Applications of Storytelling

Real-World Applications of Storytelling in Pharma Marketing

Storytelling is not just a buzzword but a powerful tool connecting science, medicine, and humanity. The best pharma stories don't just inform; they connect, inspire, and drive action.

Let's explore how storytelling is making an impact in the real world.

1. **Patient Stories: Bringing Hope and Awareness**

   Imagine you are introducing a new treatment for a rare disease. Medical data alone would not capture hearts, but a real patient's journey can.

   Example: A pharmaceutical company launches a campaign featuring a patient who struggled for years with misdiagnosis but finally found relief with a new therapy. The video follows their journey, struggles, and eventual triumph.

   Why it works:

   - Patients see themselves in the story and feel hopeful.
   - Doctors gain a deeper understanding of the real impact beyond clinical data.
   - It builds trust and an emotional connection with the brand.

2. **HCP Engagement: Making Science Relatable**

   Doctors and healthcare providers (HCPs) are bombarded with scientific data. But when you frame a story, it sticks.

   Example: Instead of a dry PowerPoint presentation on diabetes management, a pharmaceutical company shares the story of Dr. Patel, an endocrinologist who struggled to help his patients until he discovered a new treatment approach.

   Why it works:

   - It turns complex science into real-world impact.

- HCPs relate to challenges, making them more open to the message.
- It fosters peer-to-peer learning, making new treatments feel credible.

3. **Internal Storytelling: Aligning the Sales Teams**

   Your sales reps and medical teams are not just selling products but educating, guiding, and influencing. A strong brand story helps them communicate with passion and clarity.

   Example: A pharma company creates a story-driven training module where sales reps don't just learn about the product's MOA (mechanism of action) but hear real-world impact stories of how it is changing lives.

   Why it works:

   - Sales teams feel more emotionally connected to the brand.
   - They communicate with more authenticity and confidence.
   - It reinforces brand consistency across markets.

4. **Disease Awareness Campaigns: Educating Without Fear**

   Many disease awareness campaigns fail because they feel too clinical or fear-driven.

   Example: A breast cancer awareness campaign shares real-life survivor stories instead of just statistics. Women talk about their fears, diagnoses, and how early screening saved their lives.

   Why it works:

   - Instead of fear-based messaging, it inspires action.
   - It makes prevention and early detection feel personal.
   - It encourages word-of-mouth advocacy.

5. **Social Media & Digital Content: Driving Engagement**

   Storytelling on social media is not just about posting facts—it's about sparking conversations.

Example: A pharma brand uses short animated patient stories to explain how a new migraine drug works. Instead of focusing only on MOA, it shows "Emily," a working mom who regains her quality of life after finding the right treatment.

Why it Works:

- Visual + Storytelling = High engagement
- Patients feel understood and share the content.
- It makes complex medical topics digestible and memorable.

Final Thought: The Future of Pharma is Human-Centric

No matter the strategy—whether it is patient education, HCP engagement, or brand positioning—stories make everything more compelling.

What is your brand's story? Start telling it, and watch the impact unfold.

CHAPTER 10

Patient-Centric Stories

Making Healthcare Human Again

In the world of pharmaceuticals, numbers and clinical data matter. But what truly moves people—patients, doctors, even policymakers—are stories. Especially patient-centric stories, which put real people at the heart of the narrative.

Why? Behind every prescription, every diagnosis, and every breakthrough is a human being—someone battling an illness, hoping for relief, and searching for answers.

The Power of Patient Stories

Think about the difference between these two approaches:

- Traditional Pharma Messaging:

  "Our new treatment reduces HbA1c by 1.5% over six months."

- Patient-Centric Storytelling:

  "For years, Mark struggled with diabetes. No matter what he tried, his blood sugar was out of control—until he found a treatment that changed his life. Today, He is back to coaching his son's soccer team. Feeling healthier than ever."

Same message. One feels cold, the other feels human. That's the magic of patient-centric stories.

What Makes a Great Patient Story?

1. **Real People, Real Struggles**

   Great stories do not just highlight success—they acknowledge the struggle. Patients want to see themselves in the story, so showing their journey from frustration to hope makes it powerful.

2. **Emotional Connection**

   Science and facts alone don't drive action—emotions do. A well-told patient story taps into fear, hope, resilience, and relief, making it unforgettable.

3. **A Clear Before-and-After Transformation**

   A great patient story shows where the patient started, their obstacles, and how a treatment improved their lives. This transformation gives hope to other patients and credibility to the brand.

How Pharma Brands Are Using Patient Stories

- **Disease Awareness Campaigns**

  Pharma companies use real patient stories to educate people about conditions like cancer, diabetes, and rare diseases. These stories reduce stigma, encourage early diagnosis, and support newly diagnosed patients.

- **HCP Engagement**

  Doctors are more likely to remember a treatment when it is linked to a real patient experience rather than just clinical data. Sharing patient journeys helps HCPs see the human impact behind the science.

- **Social Media & Video Marketing**

  Short video testimonials, animated patient journeys, and social media posts featuring real stories are engaging, shareable, and relatable.

The Bottom Line

Patient-centric storytelling is not about selling—It's about connecting. It shifts the focus from a product to the real lives it impacts, making pharma marketing more meaningful and effective.

Your brand is not just about developing treatments. It is changing lives. Tell the stories that prove it.

Examples of Empowering Patient Narratives

Stories that Inspire Hope and Action

Patient stories are not just words on a page or testimonials in a video—they are powerful narratives of resilience, courage, and transformation. They connect on an emotional level, making complex medical journeys feel real and relatable. Let's look at some compelling examples of patient narratives that have inspired action, created awareness, and even shaped the future of healthcare.

1. **From Fear to Strength: A Cancer Survivor's Journey**

   Meet Rachel, a 36-year-old mother of two who never imagined she would face breast cancer. When she first heard the diagnosis, she was overwhelmed by fear, uncertainty, and a million "what-ifs."

   But her story did not stop at diagnosis. She found a support group, explored new treatment options, and with the help of her oncologist, she underwent targeted therapy that not only saved her life but also gave her hope. Today, she shares her journey to encourage other women to get screened early.

   Why this story matters:

   - It raises awareness about early detection.
   - It humanizes treatment by showing real-life impact.
   - It empowers other women to take charge of their health.

   Pharma companies like Roche and Pfizer have successfully used patient stories like Rachel's in breast cancer awareness campaigns, inspiring countless women to get screened.

2. **Breaking the Silence: Mental Health and Depression**

   Jake was a high-achieving executive who seemed to have it all together. Behind closed doors, though, he was battling depression and anxiety, but he was afraid to seek help because of the stigma.

Everything changed when he saw a campaign featuring real people opening up about their mental health. That gave him the courage to seek professional help, start therapy and medication, and reclaim his well-being. Today, he is an advocate, telling his story to encourage others to break the silence around mental health.

Why this story matters:

- It tackles stigma head-on and normalizes seeking help.
- It shows that recovery is possible with the right support.
- It creates a human connection to mental health treatments.

Companies like Janssen and Lundbeck have leveraged patient stories to support mental health awareness and encourage conversations about depression and anxiety treatment.

3. **Life Beyond Diabetes: Thriving with Wearable Tech**

Imagine being a 10-year-old child diagnosed with Type 1 Diabetes. For Emma, this meant daily insulin shots, constant blood sugar checks, and missing outa on spontaneous fun with friends.

Then, she was introduced to a continuous glucose monitor (CGM). Suddenly, she had real-time blood sugar data, fewer needle pricks, and more confidence in managing her diabetes. Now, Emma is a competitive athlete, proving that diabetes does not have to limit life's possibilities.

Why this story matters:

- It highlights technology's impact on patients' quality of life.
- It empowers others to see diabetes as manageable, not limiting.
- It showcases a real-world use case for innovative treatments.

Companies like Dexcom and Medtronic have used similar narratives to illustrate how medical technology changes lives.

4. **Rare but Not Forgotten: Advocacy for Rare Diseases**

   Some diseases are so rare that many patients go years without a proper diagnosis. Alex lost his young son to Spinal Muscular Atrophy (SMA) after a long and painful journey of misdiagnoses and delays. Instead of staying silent, he became an advocate, working with pharmaceutical companies and policymakers to push for early genetic screening and better access to treatment.

   Why this story matters:

   - It gives a voice to rare disease patients, who are often overlooked.
   - It influences policy and awareness campaigns.
   - It fosters a sense of community and support.

   Companies like Biogen, Sarepta, and Novartis have worked with rare disease advocates to bring patient experiences into the spotlight.

Final Thoughts: The Power of Patient Stories

These narratives go beyond just discussing medicine. They make treatments and conditions relatable, personal, and real. The best pharmaceutical storytelling is not about selling a product—it's about showing its human impact:

- Inspire action (get screened, seek treatment, stay hopeful).
- Build trust by sharing authentic, real-world experiences.
- Connect patients, caregivers, and physicians through shared journeys.

What is your story? The world is waiting to hear it.

Addressing Stigma and Bias With Stories

Breaking Barriers: How Stories Tackle Stigma in Healthcare

Stigma is a silent enemy in healthcare. It keeps people from seeking help, isolates those struggling, and creates unnecessary barriers between patients and the treatment they need. But one powerful tool can break through these barriers: stories.

Stories can shift mindsets, challenge misconceptions, and create empathy. Whether it is mental health, HIV, rare diseases, or even conditions like obesity and diabetes, real patient narratives help normalize conversations and make people feel less alone. Let's explore how storytelling dismantles stigma and opens doors for better healthcare access.

1. **Changing the Narrative Around Mental Health**

   For years, mental health struggles were whispered about—if they were talked about at all. Many people feared being labeled as "weak" or "unstable" for seeking help. But when high-profile campaigns started sharing personal stories of people battling depression, anxiety, and PTSD, perceptions started to shift.

   Take Michael Phelps, for example. The world saw him as an unstoppable Olympian, but when he opened up about his battle with depression and suicidal thoughts, it sent a clear message: mental health struggles can affect anyone, even the strongest among us.

   Why storytelling works here:

   - Normalizes mental health conversations.
   - Encourages people to seek professional help.
   - Shows that even successful individuals struggle and recover.

Companies Janssen and Lundbeck have launched mental health awareness campaigns using real patient stories, helping people see that mental illness is not a weakness—it is a health condition that deserves care.

2. **Breaking HIV Stigma with Human Faces**

   HIV was once seen as a "death sentence," and those diagnosed often faced social rejection and discrimination. But thanks to powerful storytelling, the narrative has changed.

   Take Magic Johnson. When he pubicly announced his HIV diagnosis in 1991, he used his platform to educate, reduce fear, and challenge stereotypes. Today, HIV is no longer a taboo topic, and with advancements in treatment, patients can live full, healthy lives.

   Pharma companies like Gilead and ViiV Healthcare have used real patient narratives to show that:

   - HIV is manageable with treatment.
   - People with HIV can live long, fulfilling lives.
   - There is no shame in getting tested or seeking care.

   The key? Putting real faces to the disease and proving that an HIV diagnosis does not define a person's future.

3. **Fighting Stigma Around Obesity and Diabetes**

   Obesity is often dismissed as a "lifestyle choice," and people with diabetes are frequently blamed for their condition. This stigma prevents people from seeking medical help and can make them feel ashamed of using medications like insulin or GLP-1 treatments.

   That's when storytelling makes a difference.

   Take Sarah, a woman who struggled with obesity for years. She tried countless diets, blamed herself, and felt judged every time she sought help. Then she learned that obesity is a chronic disease, not just a matter of willpower. By sharing her story, Sarah helped others realize that obesity treatments are not about "taking the easy way out"—they are about managing a complex metabolic condition.

Pharma companies like Novo Nordisk and Eli Lilly have used patient stories like Sarah's to highlight that:

- Obesity is a medical condition, not a personal failure.
- Diabetes is not just about sugar—it's about genetics, hormones, and overall health.
- Seeking medical help is not weakness; it's empowerment.

4. **Overcoming Rare Disease Stigma Through Awareness**

Rare disease patients often feel invisible. With conditions affecting only a few thousand people worldwide, many struggle to get diagnosed, find treatment, or even be taken seriously by doctors.

But when patients start sharing their journeys, things change.

For example, John Crowley's story, depicted in the movie Extraordinary Measures, shows his fight to develop a treatment for Pompe disease, a rare genetic disorder that affects his children. His journey raised awareness and accelerated research and drug development for rare diseases.

Organizations like NORD (National Organization for Rare Disorders) and companies like Biogen and Sarepta use patient storytelling to:

- Educate doctors on recognizing rare conditions early.
- Build patient communities for support.
- Push for better funding and research.

Final Thoughts: Stories Are the Bridge to Understanding

Stigma thrives in silence, but stories break that silence. When patients and advocates share their experiences, they turn fear into understanding, shame into acceptance, and hesitation into action.

The more we talk, the more we change. In pharmaceutical marketing, this means not just selling treatments but giving patients a voice that can transform their lives.

CHAPTER

11

Physician Engagement Through Storytelling

Engaging Physicians Through Storytelling: Making the Data Come Alive

Doctors are bombarded with scientific data, clinical guidelines, and drug information every day. They are trained to think logically, evaluate evidence, and make decisions based on data. But facts alone do not always drive action—stories do.

A compelling story can transform dry clinical data into something memorable, relatable, and actionable. Instead of just presenting numbers, storytelling allows physicians to see the human side of medicine— why a treatment matters, how it changes lives, and why they should care beyond the science.

Let's explore how storytelling can make physician engagement more impactful, memorable, and meaningful.

1. **From Data Overload to Emotional Connection**

   Imagine a pharmaceutical rep walks into a doctor's office and says:

   "Our drug reduces HbA1C by 1.5% and lowers cardiovascular risk by 22% in patients with Type 2 Diabetes."

   That's impressive, but will the doctor remember those numbers hours after seeing dozens of patients and skimming through medical journals? Maybe not.

Now, imagine if the rep instead said:

"Doctor, let me tell you about Sarah. She is a 52-year-old teacher with Type 2 Diabetes. She struggled with her blood sugar levels for years, trying different medications with limited success. She was exhausted, missing work, and worried about her future. But after switching to this treatment, she regained her energy, got her A1c under control, and now spends weekends hiking with her family — something she thought she would never do again."

Which version is more likely to stick? The story. Because it's not just about data—it's about real-life impact.

Why it works:

- Puts a human face to the treatment.
- Creates an emotional connection.
- Helps doctors visualize the patient's benefits beyond the numbers.

2. Simplifying Complex Science Through Narrative

Medical advancements, including gene therapy, AI-powered diagnostics, and personalized medicine, are becoming more complex. While doctors are experts in their fields, they don't always have the time to decode highly technical jargon.

A well-crafted story can translate complex science into something relatable.

Take CAR-T therapy. Instead of just explaining,

"This treatment reprograms a patient's T-cells to recognize and attack cancer cells."

Why not tell a story?

"Imagine your immune system as an army, but the soldiers don't recognize the enemy in cancer patients. CAR-T therapy acts like a special training program—it teaches the immune cells to identify and destroy cancer, giving the patient's body the power to fight back."

Suddenly, the science becomes tangible.

Why it works:

- Turns abstract science into a clear, visual concept.
- Makes new treatments easier to understand and explain to patients.
- Encourages doctors to see innovation as real-world solutions, not just theoretical advancements.

3. **Building Trust with Personal and Peer Stories**

Doctors trust science, evidence, and clinical studies, but they also trust other doctors. If they hear a peer's experience with a treatment, they are far more likely to listen.

That's why case studies, patient success stories, and doctor-to-doctor storytelling are so effective.

For example, a cardiologist may be hesitant to prescribe a new heart failure drug. But if they hear from another cardiologist,

"I had a patient struggling with worsening symptoms, and I was hesitant to try something new. However, after switching them to this new treatment, they improved significantly in weeks. Now, I use it regularly for patients who meet the criteria."

That's peer-to-peer influence in action—not just theory, but real-world success.

Why it works:

- Physicians trust their colleagues' experiences.
- Creates social proof—"If it worked for them, it might work for me."
- Reduces hesitation in prescribing new treatments.

4. **Engaging Physicians Through Digital Storytelling**

With limited time and more interactions shifting online, pharma must rethink how it tells stories digitally. That means:

- Short, engaging videos featuring real patient experiences.
- Interactive case studies where doctors can "choose" treatment paths.
- Podcasts and webinars where leading physicians discuss best practices through real stories.

Instead of a static PowerPoint with bullet points, imagine an interactive patient journey map in which doctors follow a patient's story, see decision points, and explore real-world outcomes. That's story-driven education in action.

Why it works:

- Fits into doctors' busy schedules.
- Makes learning more engaging and immersive.
- Helps them remember key takeaways better than traditional presentations.

Final Thoughts: Make the Science Stick with Stories

Doctors are driven by evidence, but they are also human. They connect deeply with patient stories, real-world experiences, and peer insights. Storytelling in pharma marketing is not about replacing data—it's about bringing it to life.

By weaving storytelling into physician engagement strategies, pharma can cut through the noise, build trust, and inspire action—one compelling story at a time.

Crafting Stories for Healthcare Professionals

Healthcare professionals (HCPs) are natural skeptics. They are trained to rely on evidence, clinical data, and logical reasoning. So, when engaging them, a brand story can't just be emotionally compelling—it has to be credible, relevant, and backed by science.

The challenge is that facts alone don't always stick. That's where storytelling comes in. A well-crafted story makes complex science memorable, turns statistics into real-world impact, and helps HCPs see the patient beyond the prescription.

Let's break down how to craft powerful stories that resonate with HCPs, inspire action, and drive better patient outcomes.

1. **Know Your Audience: What Do HCPs Care About?**

   Before crafting a story, ask:

   - What do they need? (Better patient outcomes, clinical efficiency, adherence solutions?)
   - What are their biggest pain points? (Time constraints, treatment resistance, patient engagement?)
   - What motivates them? (Improving lives, advancing science, personal career growth?)

   For example, an oncologist might care about new targeted therapies, while a primary care physician might need better ways to manage chronic disease in busy clinics. The story should be tailored to their world.

   Rule of Thumb: A great story is not just always about your product—it's about how it solves an HCP's challenges in real life.

2. **Start with a Relatable, Patient-Centric Hook?**

   HCPs think in cases, not commercials. A generic marketing message like "Our drug is the most effective in its class!" would not cut it. Instead, start with a real-world patient scenario they would recognize:

- **Before**: "A 48-year-old woman with severe asthma has been using multiple inhalers but still experiences daily symptoms. She is frustrated, missing work, and struggling to stay active.
- **After**: "After starting (Drug X), she finally controls her symptoms, enjoys walks with her kids, and no longer dreads every breath."

This kind of story works because it aligns with how HCPs think-problem, intervention, and outcome.

Why it works:

- Grounds the message in clinical reality.
- Engages HCPs emotionally and logically.
- Demonstrates patient impact beyond just numbers.

3. **Use Science, but Make it Digestible**

Yes, doctors want data, but they don't have time to sift through dense clinical papers. Your story should highlight the key takeaway in a clear and relevant way.

- **Don't**: "In a double-blind, placebo-controlled study with 5,000 patients, Drug X demonstrated a 27% relative risk in exacerbations compared to standard of care."
- **Do**: "Patients on Drug X had significantly few flare-ups, meaning they spent more time living life and less time in the hospital."

Then, back it up with a key data point: "In fact, they had 27% fewer exacerbations compared to the standard of care."

Remember: Lead with patient benefit, then support it with science, not the other way around.

4. **Keep it Peer-Driven: HCPs Trust Other HCPs**

Physicians trust clinical data, but trust their peers' experiences even more. That's why doctor-to-doctor storytelling is so powerful.

Instead of a company rep saying, "This treatment is a game changer," imagine a respected cardiologist sharing:

"I was hesitant at first, but after using this treatment with my high-risk patients, I saw remarkable improvements—especially in those who had exhausted other options."

A peer's real-world experience carries far more weight than a marketing claim.

How to do this:

- Use case studies from real practitioners.
- Feature expert interviews, testimonials, and advisory boards.
- Create roundtable discussions and webinars where HCPs exchange insights.

5. **Tailor Stories for Different HCPs**

Not all healthcare professionals have the same priorities. A specialist might not resonate with a general practitioner.

- For a specialist: Focus on cutting-edge innovation, clinical trial results, and advanced mechanisms of action.
- For a GP or nurse, Focus on ease of use, patient adherence, and quality-of-life improvements.

Example:

- A pulmonologist may want to know how a new inhaler works at the cellular level.
- A primary care physician may want to know how it fits into their daily prescribing routine.
- A pharmacist may want to know how it impacts adherence and side effects.

Same product, different storytelling approach.

6. **Make it Digital and Interactive**

HCPs have limited time—your story should be accessible in formats they prefer:

- Short, engaging videos (patient journeys, doctor testimonials).
- Interactive case studies (where they can choose different treatment paths).

- Podcasts and webinars (where they hear stories from experts in their field).

Instead of the static slide deck, imagine an interactive tool where an HCP can:

- Select a patient profile.
- Follow their treatment journey.
- See the clinical impact of different choices.

This makes storytelling more engaging, immersive, and memorable.

Final Takeaway: Science + Story = Impact

HCPs don't just want another sales pitch—they want insights, clinical relevance, and real-world impact. A well-crafted story bridges the gap between hard data and human experience, helping them understand why it matters.

By blending evidence-based medicine with compelling narratives, pharmaceutical companies can engage HCPs in a credible, memorable, and action-inspiring way, ultimately leading to better decision-making and patient care.

Bridging the Gap Between Science and Emotion

The Art of Meaningful Storytelling

Science is precise, built on data, clinical trials, mechanisms of action, and statistical significance. Emotion, on the other hand, is human, raw, and deeply personal. At first glance, these two worlds might seem like opposites. But in reality, the most powerful stories in pharmaceutical marketing sit right at their intersection.

Think about it: Physicians rely on evidence-based medicine but are driven by a desire to improve lives. Patients want the best treatment, but also crave hope, understanding, and connection. A brand that successfully blends scientific credibility with emotional resonance becomes more than just a name—it becomes a trusted partner in care.

So, how do you bridge the gap between cold, hard science and deeply felt human emotions? Let us explore how.

1. **Start with the Human Impact, Then Back it Up with Science.**

   Fact: People don't remember numbers; they remember how those numbers affect real people.

   Imagine trying to communicate the success of a groundbreaking oncology drug. You could lead with:

   "In a clinical trial of 2,000 patients, Drug X reduced tumor progression by 42%."

   That's impressive—but does it resonate? Instead, start with a real patient story:

   "When Sarah, a 43-year-old mother of two, was diagnosed with advanced lung cancer, her doctors gave her only months to live. She tried every available treatment with little success. Then, she stated Drug X. Today, three years later, she is watching her kids grow up, going on family vacations, and living life on her terms.

Now, follow it up with:

"And Sarah's story is not unique—42% of patients in a major clinical trial saw their disease progression slow dramatically, giving them more time with loved ones."

- **Why it works**:
- Leads with an emotional hook.
- Personalizes the science.
- Makes the data meaningful.

2. **Translate Complex Science into Relatable, Everyday Language**

Ever heard a scientist explain a concept in a way that only other scientists can understand? It's easy to get lost in the jargon, but effective storytelling means making complex ideas accessible and relatable.

Take, for example, a new biologic therapy for rheumatoid arthritis. Instead of saying:

"This monoclonal antibody inhibits TNF-alpha, reducing inflammatory cytokine activity and modulating the immune response."

Try this:

"Think of your immune system as a fire alarm that never turns off, causing constant inflammation and pain. This treatment works like a reset button, calming the immune system so patients can move, work, and live without constant discomfort."

- **Why it works**:
- It uses a relatable analogy.
- Strips away unnecessary jargon.
- Focuses on the patient experience.

3. **Engage Both the Rational and Emotional Brain**

Neuroscience tells us that our brains are wired for storytelling. Emotionally compelling narratives activate the limbic system (the brain's emotional center), while data and facts engage the prefrontal cortex (responsible for logic and decision-making). The key? Appeal to both.

- **For physicians**:
- Start with a compelling patient case to create an emotional connection.
- Follow with hard clinical data to reinforce credibility.
- **For Patients**:
- Start with a relatable fear, frustration, or challenge.
- End with a hopeful resolution supported by science.

4. **Show, Don't Just Tell**

A story is not just words on a page—it's an experience. The more you immerse your audience, the more powerful your message.

- Instead of just saying that a new heart failure drug improves quality of life, show it:
- A short video of a grandfather who, after treatment, can finally play with his grandkids.
- A photo essay documenting a patient's journey from struggle to recovery.
- A first-person narrative from a doctor who has seen lives changed by the treatment.

Visual and experiential storytelling helps make the science feel real.

5. **Build Trust by Acknowledging the Struggles**

Great storytelling is not about painting an overly perfect picture. People connect more with honest, nuanced stories that reflect real-life struggles.

For example, if you are telling a story about a new diabetes treatment, don't just say:

"With this medicaiton, managing diabetes is easy!"

Instead, acknowledge the challenge:

"Managing diabetes is a daily battle—constant blood sugar checks, medicaiton schedules, and lifestyle changes. It's exhausting. That's why we developed Drug X—to make small but meaningful improvements that help patients live with fewer interruptions."

- **Why it works**:
- Feels real and relatable.
- Shows empathy and understanding.
- Builds credibility and trust.

Final Thought: When Science Meets Emotion, Magic Happens

At its core, pharma marketing is not just about molecules, mechanisms of action, and data—it's about real people, real struggles, and real hope. When you can balance scientific integrity with emotional connection, you transform a product story into something far more powerful:

- A story that inspires action, builds trust, and improves lives.

CHAPTER

12

Internal Brand Building with Stories

Brand building is not just about how the world sees your company—It starts within. If your own employees do not connect with your brand story, how can you expect healthcare professionals, patients, or stakeholders to?

Storytelling is a powerful tool for internal brand-building because it turns abstract values into real, relatable experiences. It creates shared purpose, strengthens company culture, and aligns teams around a vision they believe in.

Let us explore how storytelling can ignite passion, foster engagement, and help every employee, from sales reps to scientists, become a true brand ambassador.

1. **Start with "Why": The Bigger Purpose Behind the Brand**

   Every great pharma brand has a reason for being beyond just selling a drug. It exists to solve a problem, ease suffering, and improve lives. Employees need to feel that purpose, not just read it in a mission statement.

   - **Example**: Instead of saying:
     - "We are committed to innovation in oncology."
   - **Tell a story**:
     - "When we developed Drug X, we were not just formulating a new treatment—we were fighting for every father, mother, and child battling cancer. Every late night in the

lab, every regulatory hurdle, and every clinical trial setback was worth it, because today, thousands of people have more time with their loved ones."

This shift from corporate jargon to human impact makes employees feel part of something bigger than themselves.

2. **Share the Stories Behind the Science**

   Behind every pharmaceutical breakthrough is a story of persistence, passion, and innovation. Employees should know the struggles and triumphs of bringing a product to market.

   - **Example**: Instead of just stating:
     - "Our R&D team spent six years developing this treatment."
   - **Tell a story of perseverance**:
     - "The team faced countless setbacks. Early trials failed. Regulators pushed back. But our scientists refused to give up. Dr. Patel, one of our lead researchers, spent years refining the formulation, sometimes questioning whether it would ever work. Then, one day, the results came back: Patients were responding. That moment changed everything."

   When employees hear these behind-the-scenes stories, they feel pride in their work and become emotionally invested in the brand's journey.

3. **Use Patient Stories to Inspire Employees**

   Nothing reinforces a brand's impact like hearing from real people whose lives have changed because of it. Integrating patient stories into internal communications helps employees see the human side of their work.

   - **How to do it**:
     - Invite patients to share their experiences at company meetings.
     - Create short videos of patients discussing their journey.

    - Share thank-you letters from patients in internal newsletters.

- **Example**: A pharmaceutical company developing a rare disease treatment might showcase a video of a mother saying:

  "Because of this medication, my son can now run, play, and go to school like any other kid. I can't thank this team enough."

  Stories like these remind employees why their work matters beyond financial targets and market share.

4. **Equip Employees to Tell the Brand Story Themselves**

   It is not enough for leadership to share the brand story—every employee should be able to tell it. When they understand and believe in the story, they become natural brand ambassadors who spread it internally and externally.

   How to do it:

   - Conducting storytelling workshops to help employees craft their own narratives.
   - Encourage sales reps to share personal experiences of why they believe in the product.
   - Create a story library—a collection of patient stories, innovation journeys, and brand milestones that employees can refer to.

   Example: Instead of saying:

   "Our product reduces A1C levels in diabetes."

   They can say:

   "I met a patient who struggled with diabetes for years, feeling frustrated by fluctuating blood sugar levels. When he started using our medication, he finally found stability, and he told me it gave him his life back. That's why I believe in what we do."

   By giving employees real, compelling stories, you empower them to bring the brand to life in their own words.

5. Celebrate Stories of Internal Success

Brand storytelling is not only about external Impact but also about recognizing and celebrating internal heroes. Employees who go above and beyond should have their stories told, inspiring others to embody company values.

Ideas for celebrating internal stories:

- Feature employees in internal newsletters with their stories of personal perseverance.
- Recognize teams that overcome challenges in company-wide meetings.
- Share behind-the-scenes stories of a successful product launch.

Example:

Instead of announcing, "Congratulations to the sales team for exceeding targets this quarter!"

Tell the story:

Despite supply chain issues and tough competition, our sales team found innovative ways to connect with HCPs, ensuring they had the right information when they needed it. One rep, Alex, even traveled through a snowstorm to deliver materials to a physician who had been waiting for an update on our drug's latest study results. That dedication is what makes this team extraordinary."

Employees who see themselves and their colleagues as part of the brand story feel more connected, engaged, and motivated.

Final Thought: Your Best Brand Ambassadors Are Inside the Company

The most successful pharma brands are not just built through marketing campaigns—they are built through engaged, passionate employees who believe in the story they are telling.

By integrating storytelling into internal brand building, you create a culture where employees:

- Feel emotionally connected to the company's mission.
- Understand the impact of their work.
- Naturally become brand advocates, inside and outside the organization.

When employees truly believe in the brand, they don't just sell the story—they live it. That's what makes a good pharmaceutical company great.

Storytelling for Sales and Marketing Teams

The Secret Weapon for Engagement

Let's be honest— facts, figures, and clinical data alone rarely make a lasting impression. Stories do.

A great story grabs attention, makes complex science relatable, and most importantly, persuades. That's why storytelling is not just a nice-to-have skill for pharma sales and marketing teams—it's a must-have.

When you swap dry PowerPoint slides for compelling narratives, you don't just communicate. You connect. And in pharmaceuticals, where trust and credibility are everything, that connection can mean the difference between a skeptical audience and an engaged one.

Why Stories Work in Sales and Marketing

Think about the last time you sat through a scientific presentation overflowing with numbers, mechanisms of action, and statistical significance. Did any of it stick?

Now, think about the last time you heard a real patient story—maybe about someone whose life changed because of a new treatment. That story likely stayed with you because it sparked emotion, painted a picture, and made the data feel personal.

This is why storytelling is the bridge between science and persuasion. It helps sales and marketing teams:

- Make the data meaningful—instead of saying, "This drug reduces A1C levels by 1.5%," tell a story about a patient who struggled with diabetes for years and finally found stability.
- Build trust—A compelling story removes skepticism and makes HCPs and patients more receptive to your message.
- Stand out— Everyone is bombarded with marketing messages. A memorable story is what makes a brand different.

- Simplify complex science—Science can be intimidating, but a story makes it digestible and engaging.

How Sales Teams Can Use Storytelling

1. **Open with a Relatable Story, Not Just Data**

   A sales call that begins with data dumps and feature lists can feel overwhelming. But a conversation that starts with a story immediately draws the listener in.

   Instead of this:

   "Our drug has been clinically proven to lower blood pressure by 12% in patients with resistant hypertension."

   Try this:

   "Dr. Smith, I want to share a quick story with you. One of your peers, Dr. Patel, had a patient, a 58-year-old man, who had been on multiple medications for hypertension, but nothing worked. He was frustrated, and Dr. Patel was running out of options. That's when she tried our treatment. Within weeks, the patient's blood pressure finally stabilized. He told Dr. Patel it was the first time in years he felt in control of his health again. Let's talk about how this might help your patients, too."

   Why it works:

   The story makes the science real before jumping into technical details.

2. **Use the Hero's Journey for Maximum Impact**

   A great pharma sales story follows a simple structure:

   - The Challenge—The patient or HCP faced a significant problem.
   - The Struggle—They tried other treatments but did not find success.
   - The Solution—Your brand helped overcome that challenge.
   - The Transformation—The patient's or HCP's experience dramatically improved.

Example:

"One of my clients, Dr. Miller, was struggling to get adherence from her diabetes patients. No matter how often she educated them, they would not follow through with their meds. She started prescribing our medication with its unique dosing schedule. Within a few months, she noticed a difference—patients were more engaged, their A1C levels were improving, and she was not spending extra time trying to convince them to stick with the treatment."

Why it works:

It humanizes the sales pitch and shows how your product fits into real-world practice.

How Marketing Teams Can Use Storytelling

1. **Build a Brand Narrative That Goes Beyond the Product**

   People don't just buy products—they buy stories, missions, and beliefs. If your pharma brand stands for something bigger than just selling drugs, people will connect with it on a deeper level.

   Example:

   Instead of saying, "We develop breakthrough oncology treatments," tell a story about how the company was founded by a scientist who lost a loved one to cancer and vowed to make a difference.

   Why it works:

   It turns your brand into a movement, not just a manufacturer.

2. **Use Patient-Centric Stories in Campaigns**

   Nothing is more powerful in marketing than real patient experiences. When potential patients or HCPs hear about someone like them who has benefited from a treatment, they pay attention.

Example:

A pharma company running a campaign for a migraine drug could feature a real patient video:

"For years, I missed important family moments because of my migraines. I tried everything, but nothing worked. Then, my doctor recommended this new treatment. Today, I don't live in fear of the next attack— I live my life."

Why it works:

It puts the patient first, rather than just listing clinical benefits.

3. **Create an Emotional Hook in Advertising**

   Pharma ads often fall into the trap of being too clinical, showing charts, data points, and disclaimers instead of stories that make people feel something.

   Example:

   A campaign for a multiple sclerosis treatment could show a mother writing a letter to her future self, hopeful that she will be able to dance at her daughter's wedding thanks to the medication keeping her MS in check.

   Why it works:

   It makes the audience care about the outcome instead of just explaining the mechanism of action.

Bringing It All Together: Sales + Marketing Alignment

To maximize impact, sales and marketing teams should work together to create and share powerful stories.

- Sales teams can provide real-life patient and HCP success stories from the field.
- Marketing teams can craft these stories into compelling campaigns that resonate on a larger scale.
- Both teams should consistently refine and adapt storytelling based on feedback and engagement.

Final Thought: Be the Storyteller, Not Just the Messenger

In pharmaceutical sales and marketing, you are not just delivering information but crafting an experience. Whether speaking to a physician, launching a new product, or building a brand, storytelling is your most powerful tool for inspiring, engaging, and persuading.

So, the next time you have a message to share, ask yourself:

"Am I presenting facts? Or am I telling a story that will be remembered?"

Because in a world of noise, the best story always wins.

Inspiring Employees with Brand Vision

Ever noticed how some brands feel more like movements than companies? That's because they have a clear, compelling vision—one that does not just exist in boardroom slides but lives in the hearts of employees.

In pharma, where the stakes are high and the work is deeply meaningful, having a strong brand vision is not just about strategy—It's about inspiration. When employees see the bigger picture, they don't just show up for a paycheck; they show up with purpose.

Why Brand Vision Matters to Employees

Imagine two pharma reps.

- One sees their job as just another sales role, moving numbers from one spreadsheet to another.
- The other believes they are helping a child with asthma breathe easier or a cancer patient gain more time with their family.

Who do you think will be more motivated, passionate, and driven?

That's the power of a strong brand vision—it transforms everyday tasks into meaningful contributions. Employees need to see that their work is not just about selling medications; it's about changing lives.

How to Inspire Employees with Brand Vision

1. **Start with a Story, Not a Mission Statement**

   Corporate mission statements often sound...well, corporate. They are polished, full of buzzwords, and rarely spark emotion.

   Instead, tell a story that illustrates the brand vision.

   Example: Instead of saying, "Our mission is to provide innovative healthcare solutions," tell the story of why the company exists:

   "Our founder lost his father to a disease that had no effective treatment. He vowed to change that, and today, our company works every day to ensure that no family has to go through the same experience."

Why it works: People remember stories, not slogans.

2. **Connect Every Employee's Role to the Bigger Picture**

   It's easy for employees in non-customer-facing roles to feel disconnected from the impact of their work. They might think, "I am just in regulatory," or " I just handle supply chain logistics."

   But in reality, every role plays a part in delivering hope and healing.

   Example: Instead of saying,

   "Our supply chain ensures medications reach patients on time."

   Say this:

   "Because of our supply chain team's efficiency, a mother in a remote town could get a life-saving medication for her child before it was too late."

   Why it works: Employees see how their work directly impacts lives.

3. **Share Patient Stories —Make it Real**

   Numbers and KPIs are great, but nothing resonates more than a real patient's voice.

   Companies that regularly share patient stories with employees create a culture where every win feels personal.

   How to do this:

   - Host internal meetings where patients share their journeys.
   - Create videos featuring real patient experiences.
   - Send company-wide emails with "Impact Stories" from the field.

   Why it works: Employees see the human impact of their work, not just the results.

4. **Recognize Employees Who Embody the Brand Vision**

   People don't just want to hear about the vision—they want to see it in action. One of the best ways to reinforce it is by celebrating employees who bring the vision to life.

Example:

A sales rep who goes the extra mile to educate physicians on a breakthrough treatment.

A scientist who worked overtime to accelerate a life-changing drug's approval.

Spotlighting these efforts in the company-wide meetings, newsletters, or internal social media reinforces the idea that everyone contributes to the bigger mission.

Why it works: Employees feel valued and motivated to keep making an impact.

5. **Make Leaders the Storytellers-in-Chief**

   A brand vision is only as strong as the leaders who bring it to life. Employees won't feel inspired if leaders just discuss numbers and market share.

   Instead, leadership should lead with stories.

   Example: Instead of a CEO saying,

   "We are launching a new therapy for autoimmune diseases,"

   They could say:

   "I recently met a young woman who had to give up her dream job because of an autoimmune disease. She told me she feels like a prisoner in her own body. Our new therapy has the potential to change that— and that's why what we do matters."

   Why it works: Employees see leaders who believe in the mission, and that belief is contagious.

Final Thought: A Brand Vision Employees Feel, Not Just Hear

In pharmaceuticals, our work changes lives—but only if employees feel connected to that impact. The best companies do not just talk about their vision; they embed it into their culture, communication, and leadership.

Because when employees believe in the story, they don't just do their jobs—they become part of something bigger.

CHAPTER 13

The Digital Revolution and Storytelling

A New Era of Connection

Once upon a time, storytelling was simple. People gathered around fires, read newspapers, and watched TV commercials that painted vivid pictures of brands. Fast-forward to today, storytelling has become digital, dynamic, and deeply personal.

The digital revolution has not just changed how we consume content; it has transformed storytelling itself. Pharma brands that once relied on brochures and static ads are now engaging patients, physicians, and stakeholders through interactive, immersive, and AI-powered narratives.

What makes digital storytelling so powerful, and how can pharmaceutical brands use it effectively? Let's explore.

1. **Stories Are Now Interactive, Not Passive**

   Remember when storytelling was a one-way street? A company put out a message, and the audience passively received it. Not anymore.

   Today, storytelling is a conversation, not a monologue. Thanks to digital platforms, audiences engage, react, and even co-create brand narratives.

   Example: Pharma companies use chatbots and interactive patient journeys to personalize experiences. Instead of a generic webpage, patients can now walk through real-life case studies, answer questions, and receive personalized content based on their condition or interests.

Why it works: The more interactive the experience, the deeper the emotional connection.

2. **Social Media: The Storytelling Powerhouse**

   If there is one place where stories spread like wildfire, it's social media. Whether it is patient testimonials, physician insights, or behind-the-scenes brand stories, platforms like LinkedIn, Instagram, Twitter (X now), and YouTube have become the new stage for pharma storytelling.

   Example: A pharmaceutical company launches a #MyJourneyWithDiabetes campaign, in which real patients share their struggles and successes. Instead of a brand talking at its audience, the audience itself becomes the storyteller.

   Why it works: People trust real experiences more than corporate messages.

3. **AI and Personalization: Tailoring Stories Like Never Before**

   AI is changing not just how we market but also how we tell stories. With machine learning and data analytics, brands can create personalized storytelling experiences that feel uniquely relevant to each audience segment.

   Example: AI-driven content platforms can serve different video narratives to different users based on their medical history, search patterns, and engagement behavior.

   - A newly diagnosed patient might see an educational documentary-style story.
   - A caregiver might receive an emotional supportive narrative.
   - A physician might engage with a data-backed case study.

   Why it works: Personalization creates deeper engagement and stronger recall.

4. **The Rise of Video and Short-Form Content**

   The explosion of TikTok, YouTube Shorts, and Instagram Reels has proven that bite-sized stories win big. While long-form narratives still have their place, short, engaging videos are the new currency of attention.

Example: Instead of a long testimonial, a pharmaceutical company creates a 60-second animated clip that shows a patient's journey from diagnosis to recovery. The clip clearly conveys hope and support.

Why it works: People remember stories, not stats, and video makes stories unforgettable.

5. **Augmented Reality (AR) and Virtual Reality (VR): The Future of Pharma Storytelling**

   Imagine a doctor stepping into a virtual simulation where they can see the impact of a new treatment on a 3D model of the human body. Or a patient using AR to visualize how a drug will interact with their system.

   This is not science fiction—it is happening now.

   Example: Some pharma brands are using VR storytelling to educate physicians on complex mechanisms of action, making learning immersive and engaging.

   Why it works: AR & VR turn storytelling into an experience.

Final Thought: The Digital Age Needs Human-Centric Stories

Technology has changed how we tell stories, but the heart of storytelling remains the same—it's about human connection. The best digital stories don't just leverage AI, social media, and immersive experiences; they tap into emotion, authenticity, and purpose.

Because in the end, whether it is told through a cave painting or a virtual reality headset, a story is always about people.

How Digital Platforms Have Transformed Storytelling

Once upon a time, storytelling was linear. Brands crafted their messages, printed them in brochures, aired them on TV, or placed them in newspapers, hoping their audience would listen. But digital platforms today make storytelling dynamic, interactive, and deeply personal.

From social media to AI-driven content, how we tell and experience stories has completely evolved. Let us explore how digital platforms have redefined storytelling and what it means for pharma marketing.

1. **From One-Way Broadcasts to Two-Way Conversations**

   Traditional storytelling was like a lecture: the brand spoke, and the audience listened. Digital platforms have flipped this model on its head.

   Now, storytelling is a dialogue—patients, physicians, and stakeholders do not just consume content; they react, respond, and even co-create stories.

   Example: A pharmaceutical company posts a patient's recovery journey on Instagram. Instead of being just a static post, the comment section fills with other patients sharing their own experiences, advice, and encouragement.

   Why it works: People trust real stories from real people, and digital platforms amplify these voices like never before.

2. **Social Media: The Storytelling Powerhouse**

   Think about how often you scroll through social media—what catches your attention? A wall of text? Probably not. A compelling story? Absolutely.

   Social media platforms have become mini storytelling theaters, allowing brands to engage audiences in real-time through:

   - Short-form videos (TikTok, Reels, YouTube Shorts)
   - Live Q&A sessions (LinkedIn, Instagram Live)

- Interactive polls & stories (Instagram, Twitter (X now)
- Patient & physician testimonials (Facebook, Reddit)

Example: A pharmaceutical company creates a Twitter (X now) thread following a real patient's journey, updating their progress as they undergo treatment. This real-time storytelling makes the brand feel human, relatable, and emotionally compelling.

Why it works: Social media transforms static brand messaging into engaging, evolving narratives.

3. **AI & Personalization: The Rise of Tailored Storytelling**

Imagine you are a physician researching a new treatment. Would you rather read a generic corporate press release or receive a personalized video case study tailored to your specialty?

AI-powered platforms now allow brands to customize storytelling based on the audience's needs, behavior, and engagement history.

Example: A website visitor researching a rare disease gets automatically shown a patient success story related to that condition, rather than a generic homepage message.

Why it works: Personalized storytelling makes the audience feel seen, heard, and valued.

4. **The Dominance of Video: A Visual Revolution**

There is a reason platforms like YouTube, TikTok, and Instagram Reels are booming—people remember stories better when they see and hear them rather than just read them.

Short, compelling videos have become one of the most powerful digital storytelling tools for patients, doctors, or internal brand teams.

Example: Instead of a boring product explainer, a pharma company produces a 60-second animated video showing how a new drug works inside the body—simple, engaging, and easy to understand.

Why it works: Visual storytelling increases comprehension and emotional impact.

5. **The Rise of Augmented and Virtual Reality**

   Storytelling is no longer about words and videos—It's about immersive experiences. Augmented Reality (AR) and Virtual Reality (VR) allow brands to take storytelling to a whole new level.

   Example: A pharmaceutical brand creates a VR experience where doctors can step inside a virtual human body and see how a drug interacts with cells in real-time.

   Why it works: Instead of explaining a concept, AR & VR let people experience it firsthand.

Final Thought: The Future of Digital Storytelling is Human-Centric

Technology has changed how we tell stories, but storytelling is still, at its core, about connection, empathy, and trust.

Digital platforms give pharma marketers an unprecedented opportunity to craft stories that resonate deeply with audiences through social media, AI-driven content, or immersive experiences.

Because at the end of the day, the best stories are not just told. They are felt.

Social Media and Viral Story Campaigns

If social media has proven one thing, it is that a single story can reach millions in a matter of hours when told the right way. From hashtags to heartwarming testimonials, social media has transformed how brands, including pharmaceutical companies, engage their audiences.

But what makes a story go viral? How can pharmaceutical brands use social media storytelling effectively while remaining compliant? Let's explore.

1. **The Viral Effect: Why Some Stories Explode Online**

   Going viral is not just about luck—it's about tapping into human emotions. Stories that spread like wildfire usually evoke one (or more) of the following:

   - Inspiration—Overcoming adversity, breakthrough innovations, patient success stories
   - Empathy—Emotional patient journeys, the real-life impact of a treatment
   - Shock & Awe—Surprising discoveries, groundbreaking medical achievements
   - Reliability—Everyday struggles and victories that resonate deeply

   Example: A pharma brand shares a TikTok video of a young girl with cystic fibrosis taking her first deep breath after a breakthrough treatment. The emotional impact leads to millions of shares, media coverage, and brand awareness.

   Why it works: People share stories that move them, inspire them, or make them feel connected to something bigger.

2. **Social Media: A Storytelling Playground for Pharma**

   Pharma brands once hesitated to embrace social media, fearing regulations and compliance risks. But today, they have learned how to navigate this space strategically, leveraging the right platforms to share authentic, impactful, and compliant stories.

Where the magic happens:

- Twitter/X: Quick updates, real-time discussions, physician engagement
- LinkedIn: Thought leadership, case studies, medical advancements
- Instagram & Facebook: Visual storytelling, patient narratives, behind-the-scenes content
- TikTok & YouTube: Short-form and long-form video storytelling, educational content

Example: A LinkedIn campaign by a pharmaceutical company shares behind-the-scenes stories of researchers developing a new cancer drug, making science more human and relatable.

Why it works: Social media allows brands to show, not just tell, making pharma feel less corporate, more personal.

3. **Hashtags & Challenges: The Secret to Viral Pharma Campaigns**

A well-crafted hashtag campaign can turn a story into a movement. When people see others participating, they are more likely to join in, spreading awareness organically.

Example: The #ShareYourVoice campaign encouraged cancer patients to share their journeys, leading to a ripple effect of inspiring stories across social media.

Why it works: When audiences become part of the story, engagement skyrockets.

4. **Influencers & Patient Advocates: The New Age Pharma Storytelling**

In today's digital world, people trust people, not corporations. That's why pharma brands are increasingly collaborating with:

- Patient advocates—Real patients who share their experiences authentically.
- Healthcare Influencers—Doctors, researchers, and medical experts who educate audiences.
- Micro-influencers—Niche voices with highly engaged followings

Example: A pharmaceutical company partners with a well-known diabetes advocate on Instagram, who shares real-life tips and experiences with the brand.

Why it works: Authentic voices build trust and deeper engagement.

5. **Storytelling with Compliance: The Pharma Balancing Act**

   Of course, pharma storytelling comes with unique challenges—ensuring all content is:

   - Accurate—No exaggerated claims
   - Ethical—No misleading information
   - Regulatory-compliant—Following FDA and industry guidelines

   How brands navigate this:

   - Real patient stories (with consent) instead of testimonials, making direct drug claims
   - Educational content explaining conditions and treatments without promoting off-label use
   - Third-party collaborations (influencers, doctors, and advocacy groups) for credibility.

   Example: Instead of saying "This drug changed my life," a compliant patient story might say: "Managing my condition has become easier with this new treatment option."

   Why it works: Storytelling can be powerful and responsible—it's all about striking the right balance.

Final Thought: The Future of Pharma Storytelling is Social

Social media has revolutionized storytelling, allowing pharmaceutical brands to connect with audiences like never before. By crafting authentic, engaging, and shareable stories, companies can build trust, inspire action, and create meaningful impact—all while staying compliant.

Because in the end, the best stories don't just sell. They connect.

CHAPTER

14

AI and Generative AI in Storytelling

Imagine a world where stories write themselves, adapting instantly to the reader, shifting tones based on emotions, and delivering hyper-personalized narratives at scale. Sounds futuristic? Not anymore. AI and Generative AI are already reshaping storytelling in ways we once only dreamed of.

For pharma marketers, this is not just about technology—it's about unlocking new ways to connect, educate, and inspire. Let's explore how AI revolutionizes storytelling and why it is a game-changer for pharma marketing.

1. **The AI-Powered Storyteller: What Can AI Do?**

   AI in storytelling is not just about automating content creation. It's about crafting meaningful, personalized, data-driven narratives that engage audiences more effectively than ever before.

   Here is how AI is making storytelling smarter:

   - *Content Generation*: AI tools like ChatGPT, Jasper, and Copy.ai can create engaging narratives in seconds.
   - *Personalization*: AI analyzes audience behavior to tailor stories that resonate with specific individuals.

- *Sentiment Analysis*: AI detects emotions in real-time, adjusting content tone accordingly.
- *Visual Storytelling*: AI-powered design tools generate compelling infographics, animations, and videos to complement stories.
- *Conversational AI*: Chatbots and virtual assistants craft interactive, story-driven experiences.

Example: A pharmaceutical company uses AI to create an interactive patient journey. In this journey, a chatbot shares real-time, personalized health advice based on a user's symptoms.

Why it works: AI makes storytelling more responsive, engaging, and data-backed, not just generic content.

2. **Generative AI: The Art of Crafting Unique Stories at Scale**

Generative AI goes beyond basic automation—it creates original, human-like narratives that evolve dynamically.

How pharma brands can use Generative AI:

- Generating patient-centric stories based on real-world data
- Crafting physician education content that adjusts to their expertise level
- Building AI-powered video scripts for making campaigns
- Creating real-time storytelling experiences for digital health

Example: A healthcare brand uses Generative AI to develop personalized cancer survivor stories, adjusting the narrative to different audiences—patients, caregivers, and doctors—to maximize relevance and impact.

Why it works: AI does not just tell one story—it tells thousands, each uniquely tailored to the audience.

3. **AI & The Power of Data-Driven Storytelling**

   AI thrives on data, turning numbers into narratives. Pharma brands have a goldmine of data—from clinical trials to patient experiences—but often struggle to translate it into compelling stories. AI bridges that gap.

   - *Predictive Storytelling*: AI anticipates what stories will resonate based on audience engagement trends.
   - *Real-Time Content Optimization*: AI fine-tunes content in real-time based on user interactions.
   - *Automated Case Studies*: AI converts complex medical data into easy-to-understand narratives.

   Example: A pharmaceutical company leverages AI to analyze social media conversations about diabetes and generates content that directly addresses patient concerns, making its messaging more relevant and timely.

   Why it works: AI listens to the audience, ensuring stories are always relevant and impactful.

4. **Ethical Storytelling: Can AI Be Trusted?**

   With great power comes great responsibility. AI-generated content must still align with:

   - Regulatory compliance—No misinformation or off-label promotion
   - Ethical storytelling—Ensuring authenticity, avoiding bias
   - Human oversight—AI should enhance, not replace, human creativity

   Example: Instead of AI fabricating a patient success story, a brand uses AI to create real testimonials and structure them into an engaging narrative.

   Why it works: AI is a tool, not a storyteller—human authenticity remains key.

5. **The Future: AI-Driven Interactive & Immersive Storytelling**

   Where is AI-powered storytelling heading? The future is all about immersive, real-time, and hyper-personalized experiences:

   Coming soon in pharma marketing:

   - AI-driven health coaches that share real-time, evolving patient narratives
   - VR-powered patient journeys, where AI crafts interactive health experiences
   - AI-generated pharma brand storytelling, dynamically adjusted based on user input

   Example: A patient with Parkinson's disease experiences a virtual reality journey, where AI adapts the storyline based on their real-time feedback, providing a deeply immersive and educational experience.

   Why it works: AI storytelling is not static— it evolves, making it more engaging than ever.

Final Thought: AI & Human Storytelling—Better Together

AI is not here to replace human storytellers but to amplify creativity, scale content, and enhance engagement. When used ethically and strategically, AI-powered storytelling can help pharmaceutical brands connect with audiences in a way that is more personal, meaningful, and impactful than ever before.

Because the best stories are not just told. They are experienced.

The Role of AI in Personalizing Narratives

Ever had the eerie feeling when an ad, article, or video speaks directly to you, like it knows exactly what you need at that moment? That's not magic. That's AI-driven personalization in action.

For pharmaceutical marketers, storytelling is no longer about crafting one-size-fits-all narratives. Instead, AI enables brands to create hyper-personalized, emotionally resonant, and data-driven stories that connect with patients, physicians, and other stakeholders.

Let's explore how AI personalizes storytelling, making it more relevant, engaging, and impactful than ever before.

1. **AI Understands the Audience Better Than Ever**

   Imagine you are launching a campaign for a new diabetes treatment. Traditionally, you would create one or two general stories and hope they resonate. AI flips this approach by analyzing:

   - Patient demographics—Age, location, lifestyle habits
   - Behavioral patterns— What content they engage with, how they navigate digital platforms
   - Emotional triggers—What kind of messaging sparks engagement or action

   Example: AI detects that young, newly diagnosed diabetics engage more with motivational stories about lifestyle changes, while long-time patients prefer scientific breakthroughs. AI then tailors storytelling accordingly.

   Why it works: Different audiences need different narratives. AI helps deliver the right story to the right person at the right time.

2. **Dynamic, Real-Time Storytelling**

   Traditional marketing relies on static campaigns. AI, however, enables real-time adjustments to stories based on audience interactions.

Example: A pharmaceutical website uses AI to customize patient stories. If a user searches for "managing side effects," the AI presents patient success stories about overcoming those challenges dynamically. If another user searches for "treatment options," the AI shifts the content focus to scientific advancements and clinical data.

Why it works: Storytelling evolves with the audience, keeping content fresh and engaging.

3. **Personalized Physician Engagement**

   Doctors have different information needs. A primary care physician (PCP) wants a quick, digestible patient success story, while an oncologist may prefer a detailed case study, backed by clinical trial data. AI personalizes content delivery based on these preferences.

   Example: AI-powered platforms track how doctors interact with medical content. A Cardiologist who reads case studies about heart failure receives recommendations for related patient journeys, while a general practitioner receives simplified, patient-friendly narratives.

   Why it works: AI ensures medical storytelling speaks the right language for each physician.

4. **AI-Powered Chatbots & Conversational Storytelling**

   Chatbots are no longer just for FAQs—they now tell personalized stories based on user interactions.

   Example: A chatbot for multiple sclerosis (MS) patients adapts responses based on a user's symptoms and emotional state. If a patient expresses frustration, the bot shares uplifting survivor stories. If the patient asks about treatment, it presents scientifically backed narratives on the latest breakthroughs.

   Why it works: AI-powered chatbots offer interactive storytelling that feels deeply personal and human-like.

5. **AI & Predictive Storytelling: Anticipating Needs Before They Arise**

   AI does not just react—it predicts. AI analyzes historical data and anticipates what kind of storytelling will resonate with different audience segments.

   Example: A pharma brand launches an AI-driven mental health campaign. Based on seasonal trends (higher anxiety during winter months), AI recommends featuring real patient success stories about overcoming seasonal depression, before patients even start searching for help.

   Why it works: Proactive storytelling builds a stronger emotional connection by addressing needs before they arise.

Final Thought: AI Makes Storytelling Personal, but the Human Touch Still Matters

AI is revolutionizing storytelling by making it more targeted, adaptive, and impactful. But here's the catch—while AI personalizes content, the authenticity of human emotions remains irreplaceable. The best approach is a balance:

- AI analyzes, personalizes, and optimizes.
- Humans bring creativity, empathy, and depth.

When AI and human storytelling work together, pharma brands can create compelling, emotionally resonant narratives that truly engage patients, doctors, and stakeholders like never before.

Case Studies of AI-Generated Stories in Marketing

AI-Generated Stories in Marketing: Case Studies That Prove the Power of AI Storytelling

AI-generated storytelling might sound futuristic, but it is already transforming marketing across industries, including pharma. From creating highly personalized patient stories to crafting emotionally compelling narratives at scale, AI is helping brands connect with their audiences in smarter, more impactful ways.

Let's explore real-world case studies of how AI-generated stories drive engagement and deliver marketing results.

1. **Case Study: AI-Generated Patient Stories for Cancer Awareness**

   Challenge: A global pharmaceutical company wanted to raise awareness about early-stage lung cancer but struggled to connect with patients who feared diagnosis and treatment.

   AI Solution: The company used AI-powered natural language processing (NLP) to analyze thousands of patient testimonials, extracting key themes around hope, resilience, and early detection. The AI then created personalized patient stories tailored to different demographics, each reflecting the concerns and emotions of its target audience.

   Results:

   - 30% increase in engagement on social media
   - Higher trust and credibility among patients who felt the stories "spoke to them"
   - More patients are inquiring about screenings, leading to earlier diagnoses

   Key Takeaway: AI helps craft patient stories that are deeply personal and emotionally engaging, even when shared with diverse audiences.

2. **Case Study: AI-Driven Storytelling for a Rare Disease Campaign**

   Challenge: A biotech firm launched a new drug for a rare genetic disorder but struggled to find real-world patient stories due to the condition's rarity.

   AI Solution: AI-generated stories were crafted using predictive and simulated narratives based on clinical trial data, historical patient experiences, and anonymized health records. The AI system created relatable, emotionally compelling digital stories that represented the patient journey, from symptom onset to treatment success, without violating patient privacy.

   Results:

   - Increased physician awareness, as doctors saw realistic patient journeys
   - Boosted online engagement with an 80% increase in website dwell time
   - Helped patients feel understood, leading to more discussions with healthcare providers

   Key Takeaway: AI-generated storytelling can fill the gaps when real-world patient stories are scarce, ensuring rare disease patients don't feel invisible.

3. **Case Study: AI-Powered Chatbots Creating Real-Time Stories for Mental Health**

   Challenge: A mental health app wanted to provide personalized emotional support for users dealing with anxiety and depression.

   AI Solution: They deployed an AI-powered chatbot that generated customized motivational stories in real-time. Based on user responses, the chatbot adjusted its storytelling:

   - If a user felt overwhelmed, it shared stories of resilience and small victories.

- If they struggled with medication side effects, it generated narratives of patients who found the right balance.

Results:

- 90% of users reported feeling "heard and understood."
- Higher retention rates, as users returned for daily check-ins
- More willingness to seek professional help, as storytelling reduced stigma

Key Takeaway: AI-generated stories, when personalized, can provide comfort, motivation, and a sense of belonging, especially in healthcare.

4. **Case Study: AI and Personalised Physician Engagement**

Challenge: A pharmaceutical brand promoting a new cardiovascular drug struggled to engage busy doctors with traditional marketing materials.

AI Solution: AI analyzed doctor preferences, past interactions, and specialties to generate customized case studies and scientific storytelling that spoke directly to each physician's interests.

- A cardiologist received a case study on a high-risk patient scenario.
- A general practitioner got a simplified success story on early intervention.

Results:

- Higher email open rates (+45%) and engagement
- Doctors spent 3x more time on the brand's medical content
- Increased interest in prescribing the drug due to targeted education

Key Takeaway: AI-generated storytelling makes scientific communication more engaging by delivering the right story to the right doctor at the right time.

Final Thought: AI Storytelling is Here to Stay—But the Human Touch Still Matters

These case studies prove that AI-generated storytelling is a game-changer in marketing, especially in pharma. AI helps create personalized, scalable, and emotionally engaging stories that resonate with patients, doctors, and stakeholders.

While AI can craft data-driven narratives, the human element remains essential. The best results come from a blend of AI efficiency and human creativity, where AI shapes the story and humans bring it to life with empathy and nuance.

The future of pharma marketing? AI-powered storytelling that is personal, impactful, and deeply human.

CHAPTER

15

Wearables and Immersive Technologies

The Future of Storytelling in Pharma

Imagine a world where a doctor does not just read about a new treatment but experiences it firsthand through a virtual patient simulation. Or where a patient managing diabetes receives not just medication reminders but also real-time biofeedback through a smart wearable that adapts to their lifestyle.

This is no longer science fiction—wearables and immersive technologies are transforming how pharmaceutical brands tell stories, engage audiences, and build deeper connections with patients and healthcare professionals.

How Wearables Are Revolutionizing Pharma Storytelling

Wearable devices—like smartwatches, fitness trackers, continuous glucose monitors (CGMs), and biosensors— are not just collecting data; they are telling real, ongoing health stories.

For Patients:

Wearables create personalized, data-driven narratives about health. For example, a patient with a heart condition using a smart ECG watch can see how their lifestyle impacts their heart in real time, reinforcing the importance of adherence to medication and healthy habits.

For Healthcare Providers:

Doctors can now see a patient's health story unfold through wearable data instead of relying solely on self-reported symptoms. This makes treatment decisions more informed, precise, and patient-centric.

For Pharma Companies:

Pharma brands can use wearable data to create authentic, real-world case studies that show how medications improve patient outcomes in daily life. This will make marketing campaigns more compelling and evidence-based.

Example:

A pharmaceutical company developing a new asthma inhaler partnered with a smart wearable that tracks air quality and lung function. They used real patient data (anonymized) to show how their product helped users in different environments, turning dry medical data into an engaging, visual story.

Immersive Technologies: Bringing Stories to Life

Virtual Reality (VR): Step Inside the Story

Imagine a doctor stepping into a VR simulation and experiencing the progression of Alzheimer's through the eyes of a patient. This kind of immersive storytelling makes the challenges of the disease deeply personal and unforgettable.

Augmented Reality (AR): Interactive, On-Demand Learning

With AR, a physician can point their phone at a medical brochure and watch a 3D animation of a drug's mechanism of action pop up. Pharma reps can use AR to turn static data into interactive, dynamic storytelling experiences.

Mixed Reality (MR): The Best of Both Worlds

Mixed Reality blends physical and digital storytelling. For example, a surgeon wearing a HoloLens can see the 3D overlay of a patient's anatomy, making complex surgical training more intuitive.

Why This Matters for Pharma Marketing

- **From Static to Dynamic Storytelling**: Traditional pharmaceutical marketing relied on brochures and websites. However, real-time health data, VR experiences, and interactive content make stories more engaging and impactful.
- **Building Deeper Emotional Connections**: When a physician experiences a patient's struggle through immersive tech, or when a patient sees their health progress via wearables, the message becomes personal, memorable, and powerful
- **Driving Behavioral Change**: A VR simulation of what uncontrolled diabetes does to the body can be far more persuasive than reading statistics. Stories that people experience firsthand are more likely to drive action.

Final Thought: The Future of Pharma Storytelling is Here

Wearables and immersive technologies are no longer just tools—they are storytelling platforms. They help pharma brands move beyond words and statistics to create real-time, interactive, and deeply human health experiences.

What's next? Maybe AI-powered wearables that adapt stories based on real-time health data. Or fully immersive virtual patient journeys tailored to individual experiences. One thing is clear—the future of storytelling in pharma is personal, experiential, and driven by technology.

Virtual and Augmented Realities in Pharma Stories

Transforming Pharma Storytelling

Imagine stepping into the shoes of a patient with Parkinson's disease, feeling the tremors and struggles firsthand. Or a doctor visualizing the impact of a new cancer therapy inside a virtual human body. These are not futuristic fantasies—virtual reality (VR) and augmented reality (AR) are revolutionizing pharma storytelling.

These immersive technologies allow pharma brands to go beyond traditional narratives and create interactive, emotional, and unforgettable experiences. Let's explore how they are reshaping storytelling in the pharmaceutical industry.

Virtual Reality (VR): Stepping inside the Story

VR immerses users in a computer-generated 3D world, making complex medical concepts tangible and experiential.

For Patients:

- VR can simulate disease experiences, helping people understand conditions like Alzheimer's, migraines, or anxiety disorders.
- It can train patients on using medical devices, such as insulin pumps or inhalers, in a fully interactive environment.
- **Example**: A VR experience designed for multiple sclerosis patients allows their families to experience the symptoms firsthand, creating empathy and deeper understanding.

For Healthcare Professionals:

- VR recreates real-life medical cases, enabling doctors to practice surgical techniques or diagnostic procedures without risk.

- Pharma companies use VR to demonstrate how new drugs interact within the body, making science more accessible and compelling.
- **Example**: A pharmaceutical company developing a new immunotherapy used VR to show doctors how the treatment activates the immune system to fight cancer, turning a complex process into a visually engaging story.

For Pharma Sales & Marketing Teams:

- VR can replace traditional product presentations with interactive experiences. Sales reps can guide doctors through a virtual walkthrough of a new drug's journey from molecule to market.
- **Example**: Instead of handing out brochures, a rep for a migraine medication company gives physicians VR headsets to experience a simulated migraine attack, helping them better empathize with their patients.

Augmented Reality (AR): Bringing Pharma Stories to Life in the Real World

Unlike VR, which immerses users in a fully virtual world, AR superimposes digital content onto the real world through smartphones, tablets, or smart glasses.

For Patients:

- AR-powered mobile apps can guide patients in taking their medications correctly.
- It can show real-time visualizations of a patient's condition, helping them better understand their health journey.
- **Example**: A dermatology brand created a VR app that lets patients scan their skin to detect potential early signs of melanoma. This makes self-examinations more engaging and educational.

For Healthcare Professionals:

- AR helps doctors visualize complex medical conditions in 3D.
- Medical trainees can use AR overlays to see organ systems and disease progression in real-time.
- **Example**: A pharmaceutical company developing a new cardiovascular drug launched an AR experience where physicians could point their phones at a poster and see a 3D animated beating heart illustrating how the drug improves blood flow.

For Pharma Sales & Brand Teams:

- AR can transform static brochures into interactive storytelling tools. When you scan a page, the drug's mechanism of action comes to life.
- Instead of PowerPoint slides, AR-powered presentations allow marketers to showcase treatments through 3D models and real-time simulations.
- **Example**: A company marketing a biologic therapy for arthritis used AR-enabled brochures that, when scanned with a smartphone, displayed a before-and-after X-ray of a patient's joints, making the treatment impact more visual and convincing.

The Future: Merging VR, AR, and AI for Hyper-Personalized Stories

As AI-driven personalization advances, pharma storytelling will become even more immersive.

Imagine:

- A patient with diabetes using AR glasses to see their real-time glucose levels overlaid onto their vision.

- A physician stepping into a VR patient journey, customized to reflect their specialty and interests.
- AI-powered AR that generates personalized medication plans by scanning a patient's health records.

Final Thought: The Power of Experiential Storytelling

VR and AR are bridging the gap between science and emotions, turning pharma stories into real-world experiences. By allowing people to see, feel, and interact with medical breakthroughs, these technologies transform how brands connect with patients, doctors, and stakeholders.

The future of pharma storytelling is not just about telling stories—it's about letting people live them.

Gamified Storytelling in Pharma

Turning Engagement into Experience

Imagine a doctor earning points for correctly diagnosing a virtual patient, a sales rep unlocking new insights through an interactive challenge, or a patient tracking their medication adherence like a personal quest. Welcome to the world of gamified storytelling!

Gamification blends the power of storytelling with game mechanics, such as points, challenges, and rewards, to create engaging and interactive experiences. In pharmaceutical marketing, this approach does not just capture attention; it educates, motivates, and inspires action in a way that traditional content simply can't.

Why Gamification Works in Pharma Storytelling

- **Engages the Audience**: People love games because they are fun and immersive. Adding storytelling to gamification makes experiences even more memorable.
- **Boosts Learning & Retention**: Gamified experiences make complex information easier to grasp and recall, whether a physician is learning about a new therapy or a patient is understanding their condition.
- **Drives Behavior Change**: Patients are more likely to adhere to treatment plans when rewarded for milestones, and sales reps engage more deeply when their learning feels like a challenge rather than a chore.

How Gamified Storytelling is Used in Pharma

1. **Engaging Healthcare Professionals**

   Pharma companies use gamified medical education to help physicians learn about new treatments through interactive case studies, diagnostic challenges, and virtual patient simulations.

Example: A company launching a new oncology drug created an interactive game for oncologists, where they had to diagnose and treat virtual cancer patients using real-world clinical data. Correct decisions unlocked additional insights, making learning engaging and practical.

2. **Empowering Patients Through Interactive Journeys**

   Patients often struggle with treatment adherence, but gamification can turn a routine regimen into an engaging challenge.

   Example: A diabetes management app gamified adherence by rewarding patients for consistently monitoring their blood sugar levels. Every successful log-in unlocked new educational content and personalized health tips.

3. **Training and Motivating Sales Teams**

   Gamification is also transforming how pharmaceutical sales teams learn and perform. Instead of traditional training manuals, companies now use interactive storytelling platforms that allow reps to navigate real-world sales scenarios.

   Example: A pharmaceutical brand created a sales training app in which reps acted as brand managers. By making strategic decisions, such as focusing on messaging or handling physician objections, they could see the impact of their choices on virtual sales performance.

4. **Public Awareness & Disease Awareness Campaigns**

   Gamification is not just for professionals—it's also a powerful tool for public health education.

   Example: A mental health awareness campaign created a mobile game in which players made daily decisions that affected their character's well-being. The game taught users about the importance of mental health management through storytelling.

The Future of Gamified Pharma Storytelling

With AI, gamified storytelling is becoming hyper-personalized. Imagine an AI-driven virtual coach guiding patients through their treatment plan and adjusting challenges based on progress. Augmented reality (AR) and virtual reality (VR) will further revolutionize gamification, allowing users to embark on interactive health journeys.

The Key takeaway? Pharma marketing is no longer just about delivering information—It's about creating, engaging, interactive, and unforgettable experiences that drive action.

Part V. Future Trends and the Road Ahead

The Next Chapter of Pharma Storytelling

The way we tell stories in pharmaceutical marketing is evolving at an unprecedented pace. What once relied on traditional advertisements and brochures has now transformed into immersive, data-driven, and interactive experiences. But where is storytelling in pharmaceutical marketing headed next?

The answer lies in the convergence of technology, personalization, and human connection.

What is Shaping the Future of Pharma Storytelling?

A. **Hyper-Personalization Powered by AI**

   Imagine a world where every healthcare professional and patient receives stories tailored to their needs, concerns, and behaviors. AI is making that possible. From adaptive content that evolves based on audience interaction to chatbots that tell interactive health stories, AI brings storytelling to life in highly personalized ways.

B. **Immersive Technologies: AR, VR, and the Metaverse**

   Storytelling is no longer limited to words and videos—It's becoming an experience. AR and VR allow pharma brands to transport users into virtual labs, patient journeys, and even molecular-level visualizations of treatments at work. The metaverse could soon host interactive patient education sessions or virtual symposiums where doctors engage in real-time storytelling with AI-driven case studies.

C. **Gamification & Interactive Storytelling**

   Patients, physicians, and sales teams no longer consume stories; they become part of them. Whether through gamified adherence programs, AI-powered sales training, or disease awareness challenges, interactive storytelling will continue blurring the lines between education and engagement.

D. **Social Media & Influencer-Driven Narratives**

   Trust in pharma has historically been a challenge, but real human stories—from patient advocates, caregivers, and healthcare professionals—are reshaping perceptions. Social media is making storytelling more community-driven, real-time, and relatable. Live Q&A sessions, influencer collaborations, and viral patient journeys will become core strategies for pharma brands to engage audiences authentically.

E. Ethical and Transparent Storytelling

As audiences become more skeptical of marketing tactics, authenticity and transparency will be key differentiators. Future pharmaceutical storytelling will prioritize ethical messaging, real-world evidence, and clear communication about treatment benefits and risks. The brands that thrive will be those that tell genuine, human-first stories that resonate beyond the sale.

The Road Ahead: Pharma's Storytelling Evolution

The future of storytelling in pharma is not just about innovation; it's about impact. As technology advances, pharma brands must balance digital transformation with emotional connection, regulation with creativity, and science with human experience.

Successful brands don't just tell stories; they create experiences that inform, engage, and inspire action.

So, as we turn the page to the next chapter of pharma marketing, the question is not whether storytelling will evolve—it's how boldly you will embrace it.

CHAPTER 16

Future Trends in Storytelling

What's Next for Pharma Marketing

Storytelling is evolving faster than ever. In pharmaceutical marketing, it's no longer just about telling stories—it's about creating immersive, personalized experiences that engage audiences on a deeper level. Looking ahead, the future of pharmaceutical storytelling will be driven by technology, authenticity, and human connection.

Let's explore the biggest trends shaping the next era of storytelling in pharma marketing.

1. **AI-Driven Personalization:** Tailoring Stories Like Never Before
    - Forget one-size-fits-all storytelling. The future is all about hyper-personalization, where AI crafts real-time, data-driven stories based on a person's unique health journey, concerns, and behaviors.
    - AI will analyze patient interactions, physician preferences, and even biometric data to create deeply relevant narratives. Imagine an AI-powered app that delivers motivational stories tailored to a person's treatment stage, boosting adherence and engagement.

2. **Augmented Reality (AR) & Virtual Reality (VR): Immersive Storytelling Takes Center Stage**
    - We are entering a world where storytelling is not just something you read or watch—it's something you experience.
    - Virtual reality (VR) will transport physicians inside the human body, allowing them to see how a drug interacts with cells in real time.
    - Augmented reality (AR) will overlay interactive patient journeys onto physical spaces, making medical education more engaging than ever.
    - This interactive storytelling is not just cool—it's a game-changer for education, training, and patient engagement.
3. **Gamification: Making Stories Interactive & Engaging**
    - Why watch a story when you can play through it? Gamification transforms how we educate, motivate, and engage audiences in pharma.
    - Imagine a physician training module designed as an interactive, branching-story game where decisions impact the outcome, making learning more effective.
    - Or a patient adherence app that rewards users with points and achievements for sticking to their treatment plans, turning their health journeys into engaging experiences.
    - Pharma brands can create memorable, behavior-changing experiences by blending storytelling with game mechanics.
4. **The Rise of Social Media & Influencer Storytelling**
    - People trust real people more than corporate messaging. That's why pharma storytelling will become more social, community-driven, and influencer-led.
    - Patient advocates will share authentic, first-person health stories, making complex medical information more relatable.

- Physicians and researchers will use short-form video platforms like TikTok, YouTube Shorts, and LinkedIn to present science in digestible, engaging narratives.
- Brands will co-create content with real-world healthcare influencers, bringing credibility and engagement to their stories.
- Pharma stories will be told in the future and shared, reshaped, and amplified by real voices.

5. **Ethical & Transparent Storytelling: Building Trust in a Skeptical World**
   - In an age where misinformation spreads fast, audiences demand honesty, transparency, and authenticity from pharma brands.
   - In the future, there will be a stronger emphasis on clear, truthful narratives about treatments that focus on both benefits and limitations.
   - Pharma will shift towards patient-first, evidence-based storytelling, ensuring messaging aligns with real-world experiences.
   - Ethical considerations, such as data privacy and informed consent in AI-driven content, will take center stage.

Brands that thrive will embrace openness and build trust through honest, human-first storytelling.

The Bottom Line: The Future of Storytelling is Human + Digital

The future of storytelling in pharmaceutical is not just about new technology—It's about using that technology to create deeper human connections.

- AI and data will personalize stories like never before.
- AR, VR, and gamification will make stories immersive and interactive.

- Social media and influencer-led content will make storytelling more authentic and relatable.
- Transparency and ethics will define how stories build trust in an industry where credibility matters most.

Pharma storytelling is poised for a revolution, and brands that embrace these trends will not just tell stories—they will change lives.

Data-Driven and Predictive Storytelling

Imagine a world where stories are not just told—they are anticipated, adapted, and personalized before the audience realizes they need them. That's exactly what data-driven and predictive storytelling brings to the future of pharma marketing.

At its core, this approach harnesses the power of big data, AI, and machine learning to create relevant, timely, engaging stories that are highly personalized to the needs of patients, physicians, and stakeholders.

How Does Data-Driven Storytelling Work?

Traditional storytelling starts with a message and finds an audience. Data-driven storytelling flips this process—it starts with audience insights and builds a narrative tailored to them.

Here is how it works:

- **Collecting Data:** Pharma companies gather insights from patient behavior, physician interactions, digital engagements, and real-world evidence.
- **Identifying Patterns:** AI scans through this data to uncover trends, pain points, and moments where a story can make the most impact.
- **Delivering Tailored Narratives:** The system crafts personalized stories, educational content, and engagement strategies based on the audience's preferences and needs.

For example, a diabetes management app might detect a patient skipping blood sugar logs. Instead of a generic reminder, the app delivers a motivational story about another patient who overcame similar challenges, boosting adherence.

Predictive Storytelling: Anticipating Needs Before They Arise

Predictive storytelling takes data-driven insights one step further. It does not just respond to behavior; it anticipates it.

- AI analyzes past behaviors to predict what a patient, doctor, or stakeholder might need next.
- Content is dynamically adjusted in real time, ensuring relevance at every touchpoint.
- Stories evolve based on user interactions, creating a continuous loop of engagement.

Example: A pharmaceutical brand tracking oncologists' prescribing behaviors may notice a shift toward targeted therapies. Instead of bombarding them with outdated sales pitches, the brand delivers a real-world case study demonstrating the latest breakthroughs in precision medicine.

Pharma Applications: Where Data Meets Emotion

The beauty of data-driven and predictive storytelling is that it bridges science and emotion, facts and feelings. Here's how it is making an impact in pharma:

- **For Physicians**: AI-driven platforms can identify knowledge gaps and deliver scientifically backed, real-time storytelling content tailored to their specialty and interest.
- **For Patients**: Apps and digital health tools use predictive storytelling to provide personalized educational content that evolves based on a patient's condition and engagement levels.
- **For Pharma Sales & Marketing**: Predictive analytics helps sales teams craft relevant narratives by understanding when a physician or stakeholder might be receptive to new information.

The Future: Real-Time, Adaptive, & Hyper-Personalized

The next frontier in pharmaceutical storytelling will be stories that adapt in real time, like a Netflix recommendation engine for healthcare narratives.

- AI-powered platforms will adjust messaging on the fly, ensuring that patients and HCPs receive the right story at the right moment in their journey.
- Machine learning will help predict regional health trends, enabling pharmaceutical brands to craft localized, culturally relevant stories.
- Pharma marketers will shift from static campaigns to dynamic, evolving story experiences.

In short, the future of storytelling in pharma is not just personalized—it's predictive, proactive, and deeply human. And that's a story worth telling.

The Ethics of AI and Storytelling in Pharma

AI-powered storytelling in pharmaceuticals is a game-changer. It helps craft personalized narratives, predict patient needs, and engage physicians with data-driven insights. But with great power comes great responsibility. Ethical questions loom large as AI plays a bigger role in shaping pharmaceutical stories.

Can AI-generated stories be trusted?

Are they transparent and free from bias?

Where do we draw the line between persuasion and manipulation?

Pharma marketers must grapple with these big questions as they embrace AI-driven storytelling.

1. **Truth vs. Manipulation: The Fine Line**

   AI can tailor hyper-personalized health stories—but should it? If AI detects that a patient responds better to emotionally driven narratives, should brands lean into that, even if it overshadows hard science?

   For example:

   - An AI system identifies that a hopeful success story about a new cancer drug resonates more than clinical data.
   - While the story is true, it might downplay potential risks, which could lead to unrealistic expectations.
   - Ethical Dilemma: Is this engaging storytelling or manipulative marketing?

   The Solution? Balance. AI-driven pharma storytelling must present a transparent picture, blending emotion with evidence.

2. **The Bias Problem: Can AI Be Truly Neutral?**

   AI learns from datasets—but if those datasets contain bias, the AI stories will be too.

- If an AI storytelling tool is trained primarily on Western clinical trials, it might overlook insights relevant to diverse patient populations.
- A drug that works well in one region may not be as effective elsewhere, yet AI might generalize success stories without accounting for variability.
- Ethical Best Practice: AI-powered storytelling should be trained on diverse, representative data to avoid reinforcing bias.

3. **Transparency: Who is Telling the Story—AI or Humans?**
   - If AI generates a compelling patient story, should audiences know it's AI-crafted?
   - Imagine a patient reading a heartfelt success story about overcoming a rare disease, only to discover later it was written entirely by AI.
   - Would this feel authentic or deceptive?
   - Best Practice: Pharma companies should disclose AI-generated stories and maintain human oversight to ensure credibility and trust.

4. **Data Privacy & Consent: The Biggest Ethical Hurdle**

   Personalized AI-driven storytelling often relies on patient data, browsing behavior, and engagement history. But who owns the data?

   - If AI analyzes a patient's online activity and suggests stories about a chronic condition they have not disclosed, does that cross a privacy line?
   - Using AI to craft hyper-targeted narratives must not violate patient consent or data privacy laws (GDPR & HIPAA).
   - Ethical Best Practice: Always ensure explicit user consent before using AI-driven insights to shape personalized pharma stories.

The Ethical Road Ahead: Human + AI = Responsible Storytelling

AI can make pharma storytelling more engaging, personalized, and impactful than ever before. But its use must be grounded in ethics, transparency, and responsibility.

Key Ethical Pillars for AI-Driven Storytelling in Pharma

- **Truthfulness**: AI-generated stories must be accurate, transparent, and science-backed.
- **Fairness**: AI should be trained on diverse data to avoid bias in storytelling.
- **Transparency**: Audiences should know when AI is involved in creating a story.
- **Privacy Protection**: Patient data must be handled ethically, securely, and with full consent.
- **Human Oversight**: AI should assist, not replace human judgment in storytelling.

The future of AI-powered storytelling in pharma is promising, but ethical guidelines are essential. Because, in healthcare, stories don't just inform—they influence decisions, shape perceptions, and ultimately, impact lives. And that responsibility must always come first.

CHAPTER 17

Leveraging Future Trends for Pharma Success

Storytelling in the Next Era

The future of pharmaceutical storytelling is not just about telling better stories—it's about experiencing them in entirely new ways. As technology evolves, pharma marketers must embrace emerging trends to create immersive, personalized, and deeply impactful narratives for patients, physicians, and stakeholders.

So, what's next? Let's explore the future of storytelling in pharma and how brands can leverage these trends for success.

1. **Hyper-personalized Storytelling with AI & Big Data**

   Forget generic messaging. Tomorrow's pharma stories will be uniquely tailored to individuals based on real-time data, preferences, and behavioral insights.

   - Imagine a diabetes patient receiving a digital health update that includes scientific facts and a story about someone who has overcome similar challenges.
   - AI will help craft and deliver these narratives at the right moment, on the right platform, and in the right tone, increasing engagement and trust.

   Actionable Insight: Pharma brands should invest in AI-powered storytelling engines that craft dynamic, patient-centric narratives in real time.

2. **Immersive Storytelling with AR, VR, & the Metaverse**

   The future of pharmaceutical storytelling is interactive. Audiences will not just listen to a story but step inside it.

   - **Virtual Reality (VR)**:
     - A neurologist can enter a virtual brain simulation to see how a new treatment works.
     - A medical student can experience a day in the life of a Parkinson's patient, building deeper empathy and understanding.
   - **Augmented Reality (AR)**:
     - Patients can scan a medication package with their phone and watch a 3D animated story about how the drug interacts with their body.
     - Sales reps can use holographic storytelling to present complex scientific concepts visually engagingly.

   Actionable Insight: Pharma brands should explore VR/AR content strategies to make scientific communication more engaging and experiential.

3. **Gamified Storytelling for Deeper Engagement**

   Games are not just for entertainment—they are an incredible tool for behavioral change, education, and engagement.

   - Imagine a game-based learning experience for physicians, where they diagnose and treat patients in a simulated environment, reinforcing key treatment pathways.
   - Or an interactive patient journey, where users unlock new health insights as they complete real-world actions, like taking medication on time or exercising.

   Actionable Insight: Pharma should invest in gamified storytelling to educate, engage, and motivate patients and healthcare professionals to change their behaviors.

4. **Ethical, AI-Driven Pharmaceutical Narratives**

   With AI writing stories, personalizing content, and predicting trends, there is a growing need for ethical storytelling guidelines.

Future AI-powered storytelling must:

- Be transparent—audiences should know that if AI helped craft a message.
- Remain ethical—AI must avoid bias and misinformation.
- Ensure patient privacy—no data misuse in hyper-personalized narratives.

Actionable Insight: Pharma brands must create ethical AI-driven storytelling policies to maintain trust and credibility.

5. **The Rise of Voice & Conversational AI Storytelling**

   "Hey Alexa, how does this drug work?"

   "Siri, tell me a success story of someone with rheumatoid arthritis."

   Voice search and conversational AI will revolutionize how pharma delivers stories.

   - AI-powered chatbots will tell engaging patient stories instead of just listing medical facts.
   - Voice-activated storytelling will become a key touchpoint for brand engagement.

   Actionable Insight: Pharma must optimize storytelling strategies for voice-based platforms to stay ahead.

The Future of Pharma Storytelling is Here— Are You Ready?

The next era of pharmaceutical marketing won't be about ads and brochures—it will be about immersive, AI-powered, and ethically-driven experiences that put patients, doctors, and stakeholders at the heart of the story.

- Pharma brands that embrace these future trends today will lead the industry tomorrow.

The question is—are you ready to tell the future's most powerful stories?

Preparing for New Storytelling Technologies

Are You Ready for the Future?

Storytelling in pharmaceuticals is evolving faster than ever. We have moved from static brochures and TV ads to AI-generated, immersive, and interactive narratives that connect with patients, doctors, and stakeholders in unprecedented ways.

But here is the big question: Is your brand ready to embrace the future of storytelling?

To stay ahead, pharmaceutical companies must prepare, experiment with, and adapt to new technologies, redefining how stories are created and shared. Let's explore this step by step.

Step 1: Embracing AI-Powered Storytelling

AI is no longer just a buzzword—it's a game-changer for content creation. From personalized patient journeys to predictive storytelling, AI can help brands craft stories that resonate with the right audience at the right time.

What this means for pharma:

- AI can generate customized patient stories based on real-world data, making them more relatable and engaging.
- Chatbots and AI assistants can tell interactive brand narratives in real-time conversations with patients and HCPs.
- Predictive AI can analyze engagement trends and suggest what stories will work best in the future.

Actionable Insight: Start experimenting with AI-powered content creation and train your teams to use AI-driven storytelling tools

Step 2: Exploring AR, VR, & the Metaverse for Immersive Storytelling

Traditional storytelling is one-dimensional, but what if patients and doctors could step inside your story?

- Virtual Reality (VR) can simulate real-world patient experiences, helping doctors understand conditions like Alzheimer's or Schizophrenia in a deeply emotional and immersive way.
- Augmented Reality (AR) can bring drug mechanisms or treatment effects to life with interactive, 3D animations—way more engaging than a PowerPoint presentation!
- The Metaverse opens up a whole new world of storytelling. Pharma brands can create virtual medical training, patient education, and brand engagement spaces.

Actionable Insight: Pharma brands should start piloting small AR/VR projects to see what resonates with their audiences.

Step 3: Leveraging Data-Driven Presentation

Storytelling is not just about what you say—it's about who you tell it to and when.

With Big Data and AI, pharma brands can personalize stories based on:

- Patient demographics & medical history—Tailoring content to a diabetes patient's journey.
- HCP preferences & engagement trends—Creating targeted education modules for specialists.
- Real-time feedback & behavior analytics—Adjusting narratives based on audience reactions.

Actionable Insight: Invest in data-driven storytelling platforms allowing real-time content adaptation and audience segmentation.

Step 4: Adapting to Voice & Conversational AI

"Hey Siri, how does this medication work?"

"Alexa, tell me a real patient success story about this treatment."

Voice search and conversational AI are the next frontiers for pharma storytelling. Instead of scrolling through articles, patients and doctors will listen to stories, interact with chatbots, and engage with AI-driven voice assistants.

Actionable Insight: Optimize storytelling for voice-based interactions and explore AI-driven chatbots for real-time engagement.

Step 5: Building Future-Ready Storytelling Culture

New technologies mean new ways of thinking. Pharma companies that embrace experimentation, agility, and cross-functional collaboration will lead the future of storytelling.

- Train teams on emerging storytelling tech.
- Partner with digital innovators to test new platforms
- Adopt a "test and learn" mindset—start small, measure impact, and scale up successful experiments.

Actionable Insight: Encourage internal innovation teams to explore new storytelling methods and platforms.

The Future is Now—Are You Ready?

Pharma storytelling is no longer about crafting messages but creating experiences. Brands that embrace new technologies today will shape the industry tomorrow.

So, what is your next step? Will you watch from the sidelines, or will you start preparing to lead the way in the next era of pharma storytelling?

Integrating Emerging Tools into Brand Strategies

New storytelling technologies are exciting, but integrating them into your brand strategy is the real challenge. It's not just about using the latest tools—it's about using them smartly and strategically to enhance engagement, build trust, and drive results.

Let's break it down into actionable steps to seamlessly weave these emerging tools into your pharma brand strategy.

Step 1: Define Your Brand's Storytelling Goals

Before diving into AI, VR, or social listening, take a step back and ask:

- What is the core message we want to tell?
- Who are we speaking to—patients, HCPs, or both?
- How can technology enhance—not replace—the emotional power of our stories?

Actionable Insight: Align emerging tools with your existing brand vision to ensure they support your long-term strategy.

Step 2: Leverage AI for Smarter, Data-Driven Storytelling

AI is not just about generating content—it's about making it personal, timely, and effective.

- Personalized Patient Journeys—AI can craft individualized narratives based on a patient's condition, treatment stage, or concerns.
- Predictive Content Planning—AI can analyze past engagement trends to suggest which stories resonate most.

Actionable Insight: Start small. Use AI to analyze audience engagement and optimize your existing content before moving into AI-generated storytelling.

Step 3: Embrace AR & VR for Immersive Brand Experiences

Why tell a story when you can let your audience experience it?

- For patients—Use VR to simulate what it is like living with a condition, helping them better understand symptoms and treatments.
- For HCPs—Create interactive VR experiences that bring drug mechanisms, case studies, or patient success stories to life.
- For Sales & Training—Use immersive simulations to train reps, making complex scientific data more engaging.

Actionable Insight: Start with pilot AR/VR projects at medical conferences or digital platforms, then scale up based on engagement.

Step 4: Master Social Media & Real-Time Storytelling

Social media is not just a distribution channel—it's where stories come to life in real-time.

- Micro-Stories & Snackable Content—Short, engaging formats (TikTok, Instagram Reels, LinkedIn shorts) can break complex topics into digestible pieces.
- Live Storytelling—Webinars, live Q&As, and Twitter (X now) Spaces allow real-time engagement between patients, experts, and brand leaders.
- Influencer & Patient Ambassadors—Authentic voices—patients, doctors, or scientists— make pharma stories more relatable.

Action Insight: Build a content ecosystem that blends long-form storytelling with social-first, interactive experiences.

Step 5: Integrate Conversational AI & Voice Search

With more people using voice search and smart assistants, pharma brands must optimize storytelling for these platforms.

- Voice-Optimized FAQs & Narratives—Patients should be able to ask "Alexa, what's the story behind this treatment?" And get an engaging response.

- AI-driven Chatbots—Imagine a conversational AI assistant guiding patients through treatment options or helping HCPs explore clinical data.
- Podcast-Style Audio Stories—On-the-go storytelling through branded health podcasts or AI-generated patient narratives.

Actionable Insight: Test voice-driven interactions by optimizing existing content for voice search and exploring AI chatbots for engagement.

Step 6: Make Data-Driven Decisions for Continuous Optimization

New tools mean new data points—but raw data alone won't help unless you analyze and act on it.

- Track What Works—AI tools can measure engagement, sentiment, and effectiveness of different storytelling formats.
- Refine & Iterate—Use A/B testing to determine which stories connect best with different audiences.
- Personalized Story Adaptation—Dynamic content can evolve in real-time based on patient/HCP feedback.

Actionable Insight: Implement real-time analytics dashboards to refine storytelling strategies based on audience response continuously.

The Takeaway: Smart Integration, Not Just Trend Adoption

The future of pharma storytelling is not about adapting every shiny new tool—it's about integrating the right technologies to enhance your brand's story, connect deeply with audiences, and drive impact.

So, where will you start? Will you use AI for personalization, AR for engagement, or voice tech for accessibility? Whatever you choose, the key is thoughtful, strategic integration. Because the brands that tell the best stories don't just follow trends—they create them.

Part VI. Resources and Case Studies

Bringing Stories to Life

So, you have explored the power of storytelling in pharma marketing—from crafting compelling narratives to integrating cutting-edge technologies. But theory alone is not enough. Now, it's time to see real-world applications in action.

This final section explores case studies and resources to help you move from inspiration to execution. You will discover how top pharma brands, healthcare organizations, and even unexpected players have used storytelling to engage patients, connect with HCPs, and build trust in an industry where credibility is everything.

Let's explore what worked, what did not, and what you can learn from these success stories.

What You Will Find in This Section

1. **Case Studies of Pharma Storytelling in Action**
   - How leading brands used patient narratives, digital storytelling, and AI-driven engagement to transform their marketing.
   - Real-world examples of storytelling in pharma sales, physician engagement, and internal brand building.
2. **Lessons from Other Industries**
   - What pharma can learn from automotive, tech, and retail brands that have mastered the art of storytelling.
3. **Tools & Resources to Get Started**
   - A curated list of books, online courses, content creation platforms, and AI-driven storytelling tools.
4. **A Step-by-Step Action Plan**
   - Practical, easy-to-follow steps to help you apply what you have learned and craft your pharma storytelling strategy.

Why This Matters

You don't need to reinvent the wheel. Great storytelling strategies already exist. By studying successful case studies and leveraging the right resources, you can accelerate your storytelling journey and create impactful narratives that resonate with patients, physicians, and stakeholders.

CHAPTER

18

Case Studies of Successful Storytelling in Pharma

Pharma marketing is not just about data, efficacy, and clinical claims—It's about stories that make people feel something. The most successful pharmaceutical brands don't just sell products; they create narratives that educate, inspire, and build trust with patients, physicians, and the healthcare community.

Let's look at real-world examples where storytelling made all the difference.

1. **GSK's "#AskAboutAsthma"—Educating Through Personal Stories**

   The Challenge:

   Asthma is a common yet underestimated condition. Many people, especially parents, don't realize the importance of proactive asthma management until a crisis occurs. GSK wanted to change that by encouraging early intervention and better patient-doctor conversations.

   The Storytelling Approach:

   GSK raised awareness by using patient-driven storytelling instead of data-heavy campaigns. They launched #AskAboutAsthma, a digital and social media initiative in which real asthma patients, caregivers, and healthcare professionals shared their experiences.

- *Personal Stories*: Young people living with asthma described their struggles—missing school, avoiding sports, and facing unexpected attacks. Their stories highlighted the real-life impact of poorly managed asthma.
- *Empowering Messaging*: Instead of fear-based communication, the campaign encouraged proactive steps: asking doctors about inhaler techniques. Recognizing early symptoms and understanding trigger management.
- *Multi-Channel Strategy*: Stories were shared through videos, blogs, and social media, ensuring widespread reach.

The Impact:

- *Higher Engagement*: Social media conversations around asthma awareness surged, with parents and patients sharing their stories.
- *Behavioral Change*: More parents reported taking their children for early check-ups and preventive care.
- *Increased Trust in GSK*: By focusing on patient needs rather than pushing a product, GSK reinforced its role as a patient-centric company.

2. **Novartis' "The Story of a Gene Mutation"—Making Science Relatable**

The Challenge:

Rare genetic disorders, including certain types of epilepsy, often seem like abstract, clinical conditions. Families affected by these diseases can feel isolated, and public awareness remains low. Novartis wanted to humanize the impact of genetic research.

The Storytelling Approach:

- Novartis created an emotional yet informative campaign, blending real patient stories with cutting-edge scientific explanations.

- *Real Faces of the Disease*: Instead of focusing solely on data, Novartis shared the stories of children diagnosed with rare gene mutations. Parents spoke about their journey—how they struggled to find a diagnosis, the fear of the unknown, and how science eventually provided the answers.
- *Science Simplified*: The campaign included short animations explaining how gene mutations lead to disorders, breaking down complex medical concepts into simple, engaging narratives.
- *Physician and Researcher Voices*: Leading scientists and doctors spoke about their passion for finding a cure, making research more relatable.

Impact:

- *Greater Patient Advocacy*: Parents of children with rare disorders became vocal about their experiences, helping others find support.
- *Increased Research Interest*: Scientists and healthcare professionals engaged more with the campaign, strengthening collaborations for future research.
- *Stronger Brand Trust*: Novartis positioned itself as a champion for rare disease awareness, reinforcing its credibility in genetic research.

3. **Pfizer's "Before it Became a Medicine"—Humanizing Drug Development**

The Challenge:

Many people don't understand the long, complex process of drug development. Some people are skeptical about pharmaceutical companies, believing they prioritize profits over patients. Pfizer aimed to increase transparency and rebuild trust.

The Storytelling Approach:

Pfizer launched "Before it Became a Medicine," a documentary-style campaign that revealed the real, behind-the-scenes journey of drug development.

- *Real Scientists, Real Struggles*: Pfizer featured actual scientists who worked on life-saving drugs instead of using actors. They spoke about the years of research, the many failures, and their investment in every project.
- *Patient Testimonials*: The campaign also highlighted patients who benefited from newly developed drugs, making the connection between science and human lives.
- *Interactive Website*: A dedicated digital platform allowed viewers to explore different stages of drug development, from discovery to regulatory approval.

The Impact:

Improved Public Perception: The campaign helped counter misinformation about pharmaceutical companies and the drug approval process.

- *Higher Engagement*: Patients and medical professionals engaged with the campaign, sharing it across platforms.
- *Stronger Brand Loyalty*: Pfizer reinforced trust among healthcare providers and the general public by being transparent about its process.

4. **Sanofi's "Diabetes Your Type"—Personalizing Patient Journeys**

The Challenge:

Diabetes is not a one-size-fits-all condition. Many patients feel frustrated when prescribed generic treatment plans that don't align with their needs. Sanofi wanted to emphasize personalized diabetes care and encourage patient-doctor discussions.

The Storytelling Approach:

Sanofi developed "Diabetes Your Type," a campaign that shared diverse patient experiences to show that every diabetes journey differs.

- *Multiple Patient Stories*: The campaign featured young athletes, working professionals, and elderly patients, each with a unique experience of managing diabetes.
- *Lifestyle-Focused Messaging*: Instead of solely talking about insulin and medication, the stories focused on daily challenges, such as diet, exercise, and mental health.
- *Empowering Call to Action*: Patients were encouraged to speak to their doctors about personalized treatment options, moving beyond a "one-treatment-fits-all" approach.

Impact:

- *More Informed Patients*: The campaign led to more doctor-patient conversations about personalized care.
- *Shift in Diabetes Management Approach*: Healthcare providers started emphasizing tailored treatment plans, recognizing that diabetes management should be individualized.
- *Brand Credibility*: Sanofi strengthened its image as a patient-first company that understands diabetes management.

Key Takeaways: Why These Stories Worked

1. Authenticity Matters—Real patient voices, unfiltered experiences, and genuine emotions make storytelling powerful.
2. Education Through Emotion—Combining scientific explanations with relatable stories makes complex information digestible.
3. Multi-Channel Approach Wins—Leveraging social media, videos, websites, and real-world events ensures maximum impact.

4. Call to Action is Essential—Stories should inform and empower people to take action, whether seeking early care, understanding science, or engaging in discussions.

These real-world examples highlight how storytelling in pharma marketing is evolving beyond product promotion to meaningful, patient-centered communication. The future belongs to brands that master the art of blending science with human experience, creating narratives that resonate, educate, and inspire.

Real-World Examples and Outcomes

Storytelling is not just about spinning a good tale—it's about creating meaningful connections. In pharma marketing, where trust, science, and emotions intersect, real-world examples show how powerful narratives can shape patient perceptions, enhance physician engagement, and ultimately drive better health outcomes.

Let's explore some compelling cases where storytelling made all the difference.

1. **GSK's "#AskAboutAsthma"—Empowering Patients with Awareness**

   Asthma management is often overlooked until an emergency strikes. To change that, GSK supported the #AskAboutAsthma campaign, which used real patient stories to emphasize the importance of proactive asthma care. The campaign encouraged parents and caregivers to ask the right questions and take preventive steps by featuring young asthma patients sharing their struggles and triumphs. Outcome? Increased awareness and a rise in early interventions, helping children manage asthma better.

2. **Novartis' and "The Story of a Gene Mutation"—Bridging Science and Emotion**

   Genetic disorders often seem like abstract medical conditions until real people share their experiences. Novartis used storytelling to humanize epilepsy research, showcasing families affected by rare genetic mutations. They combined patient testimonials with expert insights, making complex science more relatable. Result? A surge in public interest and engagement, sparking conversations among researchers, patients, and advocacy groups.

3. **Pfizer's "Before it Became a Medicine"—Demystifying Drug Development**

   Most people don't realize the decade-long journey a drug takes before reaching patients. Pfizer's "Before it Became a Medicine" campaign pulled the curtain on clinical trials, failures, and breakthroughs, using real scientists and patients in their storytelling. Impact? It built credibility, educated the public, and positioned Pfizer as a brand that values transparency in medicine.

4. **Sanofi's "Diabetes Your Type"—Personalizing Patient Care**

   Diabetes is not a one-size-fits-all disease. Sanofi's "Diabetes Your Type" campaign featured real patients discussing their struggles, emphasizing the importance of personalized treatment plans. Outcome? Increased patient engagement with healthcare providers and a shift towards individualized diabetes care.

   Each of these examples proves that storytelling in pharmaceuticals is not about marketing—it's about making science human. Pharmaceutical brands build trust, drive engagement, and contribute to better healthcare outcomes by crafting authentic, patient-centric narratives.

Lessons Learned from Industry Leaders

If there is one thing the pharmaceutical industry has learned, it is that facts alone don't change minds—stories do. The most successful pharma brands have realized that science must be woven into human narratives to truly connect with patients, healthcare providers, and the public. Let's explore some of the biggest lessons industry leaders have learned while mastering the art of storytelling.

1. **Authenticity is Everything—Patients Can Spot Marketing Hype**

   Lessons from: Pfizer's "Science Will Win" Campaign

   Pharmaceutical companies were under intense scrutiny when the world anxiously awaited COVID-19 vaccines. Instead of a traditional PR approach, Pfizer put scientists at the forefront, sharing their relentless dedication to research and breakthroughs.

   What we learned:

   - People trust real, unscripted stories.
   - Instead of over-polished corporate messaging, brands should showcase the people behind the innovation.
   - Featuring real researchers, patients, and healthcare professionals creates credibility and an emotional connection.

   Takeaway: Show the heart behind the science. Let patients and researchers tell their stories in their own words—without corporate spin.

2. **Storytelling Should Educate, Not Just Sell**

   Lessons from: Novartis' "The Story of a Gene Mutation"

   Novartis could have discussed drug efficacy in cold, clinical terms. Instead, it used storytelling to educate patients and physicians about genetic mutations, making complex science accessible through animations and real patient stories.

What we learned:

- Storytelling is a tool for education—it's not just about selling a product.
- Breaking down complex topics into relatable, engaging narratives helps patients and healthcare professionals better understand diseases and treatments.
- Visual storytelling (animations, illustrations, and videos) makes scientific concepts more digestible.

Takeaway: Think beyond product promotion—tell stories that make science meaningful and accessible.

3. **Multi-Channel Storytelling Drives Deeper Engagement**

Lessons from Sanofi's "Diabetes Your Type" Campaign

Sanofi understood that diabetes is not a one-size-fits-all disease. Thus, they launched "Diabetes Your Type," a multi-platform campaign featuring personal stories in video, social media, and interactive content. The narratives allow patients to see themselves reflected in the campaign.

What we learned:

- The same story can be told in different ways depending on the platform.
- Social media thrives on bite-sized storytelling, while longer formats like videos or articles allow for deeper emotional engagement.
- Omnichannel storytelling ensures broader reach and impact.

Takeaway: Your audience is everywhere, so make sure your story is, too. Adapt narratives for different platforms while keeping the message consistent.

4. **Personalization is the Future—AI Can Help**

   Lessons from: Roche's Personalized Patient Support Programs

   Roche has been a pioneer in leveraging AI-driven storytelling, tailoring content to individual patient needs. Their AI-powered patient support programs provide customized guidance based on each patient's journey, making their messaging feel deeply personal and relevant.

   What we learned:

   - Personalization increases engagement and trust—patients resonate more with stories tailored to them.
   - AI can help brands deliver the right story to the right person at the right time.
   - Chatbots, recommendation engines, and predictive analytics can make storytelling more interactive and dynamic.

   Takeaway: AI is not just a tech buzzword. It's revolutionizing how pharmaceutical brands tell stories; personalized storytelling is the next frontier.

5. **Community-Driven Storytelling Builds Brand Loyalty**

   Lessons from: GSK's #AskAboutAsthma Campaign

   Instead of a top-down approach, GSK empowered real patients and caregivers to drive the conversation around asthma awareness. They turned patients into brand advocates by amplifying user-generated content and community stories.

   What we Learned:

   - When people see others like them sharing experiences, they are more likely to engage and take action.
   - Community-driven storytelling fosters trust and loyalty.

- Instead of just broadcasting messages, brands should create platforms for patients to share their stories.

Takeaway: People trust people more than brands. Give them a voice; your brand will benefit from genuine, organic content.

Final Thoughts: The Road Ahead

The most powerful pharmaceutical brands are no longer science-driven—they are story-driven. Industry leaders have learned that the future of pharmaceutical marketing is not about pushing products but about crafting meaningful, educational, and authentic narratives that truly connect with people on a human level.

The question now is not if pharma brands should embrace storytelling—it is how well they can master it.

CHAPTER

19

The Storytelling Toolkit for Pharma Marketers

In today's pharmaceutical world, a well-told story can be more powerful than the most data-packed presentation. Storytelling is not just about crafting a compelling narrative—it's about using the right tools to bring that narrative to life, making science accessible, engaging, and most importantly, memorable.

So, what do you need in your storytelling toolkit to truly connect with patients, healthcare professionals, and stakeholders? Let's explore.

1. **The Core Narrative: Your Story's Foundation**

   Every great pharma story needs a solid foundation. Before jumping into visuals, social media, or AI. You must answer these fundamental questions:

   - Who is the hero? (A patient? A researcher? A doctor?)
   - What challenge do they face? (A disease? Lack of awareness? Access to treatment?)
   - How does your brand help them overcome it?

   Example: Instead of saying, "Our new treatment improves lung function by 30%," tell the story of a COPD patient who struggled with everyday tasks but regained independence thanks to your innovation.

Toolkit Tip:

Use the three-act structure (Beginning: the problem, Middle: the struggle, End: the resolution) to craft a narrative that resonates.

2. **Emotional Triggers: The Science of Connection**

   People may trust the data, but they act on emotions. A good story should evoke:

   - Empathy (Show real patient struggles)
   - Hope (Highlight solutions and success stories)
   - Inspiration (Celebrate resilience and medical breakthroughs)

   Example: Instead of listing side effects and statistics, show a cancer survivor sharing their journey by ringing the victory bell after treatment.

   Toolkit Tip:

   Use sensory details—describe how a patient feels, their challenges, and the moment of relief when they find a solution.

3. **Multi-Channel Storytelling: Right Message, Right Place**

   Different audiences engage with content in different ways. Your story should be adapted for multiple platforms while keeping a consistent core message.

   - Short-form storytelling (Social media, reels, TikTok, Twitter threads), Bite-sized patient stories, behind-the-scenes research clips
   - Long-form storytelling (Blog posts, YouTube, patient interviews, documentaries), and deep dives into success stories
   - Infographics and Visual Storytelling (Instagram, LinkedIn, medical journals), breaking down complex science into digestible, engaging content

Example: A story about a new diabetes drug can be told as a 30-second patient testimonial on Instagram, an animated explainer on YouTube, and a doctor's Q&A session on LinkedIn.

Toolkit Tip:

Use omnichannel storytelling—don't just repurpose content; tailor it for each platform.

4. **AI and Personalization: The Future of Storytelling**

AI-powered storytelling is transforming pharma marketing by personalizing content for different audiences.

- Chatbots & AI Assistants provide personalized health insights based on users' questions.
- AI-Generated Content adapts stories for different patient demographics or regional needs.
- Predictive Analytics understands what kind of stories resonate most with your audience.

Example: Roche uses AI to personalize patient education materials, ensuring that each person gets the most relevant information based on their health journey.

Toolkit Tip:

Use AI to analyze engagement data—see which stories perform best and refine your approach accordingly.

5. **Immersive Technologies: Bringing Stories to Life**

New-age storytelling is no longer just words on a page. With AR, VR, and gamification, pharma marketers can create interactive experiences that engage audiences like never before.

- Virtual Reality(VR) Patient Journeys let HCPs experience what it is like to live with a chronic illness.
- Augmented Reality (AR) Educational Tools help doctors visualize drug mechanisms in real-time.
- Gamification & Interactive Campaigns make learning about diseases and treatments more engaging for patients.

Example: Novartis used VR simulations to help doctors understand what it is like to have advanced macular degeneration, creating deeper empathy for patients.

Toolkit Tip:

Experiment with immersive storytelling makes complex medical topics more tangible and relatable.

6. **Measuring Impact: The Analytics Behind Storytelling**

A great story is only effective if it reaches and resonates with the right audience. That's where analytics come in.

- Engagement Metrics—How many people watched, liked, or shared your story?
- Sentiment Analysis—Are people reacting positively or negatively?
- Conversion Tracking—Did storytelling increase patient awareness, doctor engagement, or brand loyalty?

For example, a patient testimonial campaign might drive 20% more social shares than a traditional product ad, showing the power of storytelling in action.

Toolkit Tip:

Use A/B testing to refine your storytelling approach—experiment with different formats and narratives to see what works best.

Final Thoughts: Your Storytelling Edge

In pharmaceutical marketing, storytelling is not an add-on—it's a necessity. Brands that humanize their science, engage across multiple channels, leverage technology, and measure impact will truly connect with their audiences.

So, what's your next great pharma story going to be?

Practical Templates and Frameworks

Your Storytelling Cheat Sheet

Great storytelling in pharma marketing is not just about creativity—it's about structure. You can consistently craft compelling, impactful narratives with the right templates and frameworks. Whether you share a patient journey, explain complex science, or engage healthcare professionals (HCPs), these storytelling blueprints will help you create stick stories.

Let's explore practical storytelling frameworks you can use right away!

1. **The Patient Journey Framework: From Struggle to Success**

   Best for: Patient testimonials, awareness campaigns, and social media stories.

   This framework mirrors the real-life experience of a patient, making the story highly relatable and emotional.

   Step 1: The Challenge—Describe the patient's struggle (diagnosis delay, treatment side effects, stigma)

   Step 2: The Turning Point—introduce the treatment, brand, or innovation that changed their life.

   Step 3: The Resolution—Show the outcome (improved quality of life, regained confidence, hope)

   Example:

   "Sarah, a 32-year-old artist, struggled with severe psoriasis for years, hiding behind long sleeves and avoiding public events. After discovering a new biologic treatment, she finally found relief. Today, she is not just painting again— she confidently wears short sleeves for the first time in a decade."

Template:

"Meet [Patient Name], who battled [Condition]. Life was tough because [Pain Point]. Then, [Discovery of Treatment/Support]. Now [Positive Transformation]."

2. **The "Hero's Journey" for HCP Engagement**

Best for: Medical education, HCP training, scientific storytelling.

Doctors and healthcare professionals constantly solve problems, so why not frame your story like a hero's quest?

Step 1: The Mission—The physician's challenge (diagnosis difficulties, patient non-adherence).

Step 2: The Guide (Your Brand/Science)—How your solution provides support.

Step 3: The Victory—How the HCP successfully helps patients using your product.

Example:

"Dr. Patel struggled to find an effective treatment for his diabetic patients with chronic wounds. With a new regenerative therapy, he is helping them heal faster, reducing complications and improving their quality of life."

Template:

"Dr [Last Name] faced [Medical Challenge]. With [Brand/Treatment], they could [Positive Outcome]. Today, they are transforming patient care."

3. **The "Problem-Solution-Impact" Formula**

Best for: Disease awareness campaigns, product messaging, investor storytelling.

Step 1: The Problem—What issue are you addressing?

Step 2: The Solution—How does your innovation solve it?

Step 3: The Impact—What are the results or real-world benefits?

Example:

"Over 70% of migraine sufferers struggle to find an effective treatment. Our new migraine-targeting therapy provides rapid relief within 30 minutes, reducing attack frequency by 50%. Patients can finally get back to living life on their terms."

Template:

"[Dr of people] suffer from [Problem]. [Your Brand/Treatment] offers [Solution], leading to [Impact]."

4. **The "Before-After-Bridge" Formula for Sales & Marketing**

   Best for: Sales pitches, brand messaging, digital marketing.

   Step 1: Before—What was life like before your product existed?

   Step 2: After—What transformation happens after using it?

   Step 3: Bridge—How does your product make that change possible?

   Example:

   "Before our AI-powered patient monitoring system, hospitals struggled to detect early signs of sepsis. Now, early detection has reduced ICU admissions by 30%. Our AI-driven alerts ensure doctors intervene before it is too late.

   Template:

   "Before [Your Solution], [Pain Point]. Now [Positive Outcome]. Thanks to [Your Innovation], [Why It Works]."

5. **The "Data-Driven Story" Approach for Pharma Innovation**

   Best for: Clinical trial results, investor presentations, regulatory submissions.

   Step 1: The Research Insight—Introduce a key scientific finding.

   Step 2: The Human Connection—Show how this data impacts real lives.

Step 3: The Future Implication—Explain what this means for patients and medicine.

Example:

Clinical trials show that our new gene therapy reduces rare blood disorder symptoms by 85%. For young patients like Mia, this means fewer hospital visits and a future filled with possibilities."

Template:

"A recent study found that [Scientific Insight]. This means [Real-World Impact] for [Target Audience]. Looking ahead, [Future Implication]."

Final Thoughts: Your Story, Your Impact

These plug-and-play storytelling frameworks can help you craft resonant pharma stories—whether you are talking to patients, doctors, investors, or the public. By structuring your message effectively, you can make complex science engaging, memorable, and actionable.

So, which framework are you are using for your next powerful pharma story?

Tools for Crafting and Measuring Stories

Your Pharma Storytelling Toolkit

Telling a great story is an art, but measuring its impact is a science in pharmaceutical marketing. Every message must be credible, compelling, and compliant. Having the right tools can make all the difference.

So, let's explore some of the best tools and technologies that can help you craft powerful pharma stories and track their effectiveness in a way that drives results.

1. **Tools for Crafting Pharma Stories**
   - **AI-Powered Writing Assistants**
     - Grammarly & Hemingway Editor— Ensures your story is clear, concise, and engaging. Helps simplify complex medical jargon for HCPs and patients alike.
     - ChatGPT & Jasper— AI-driven platforms that help generate story ideas, refine messaging, and adapt content for different audiences.
     - Notion & Evernote— Great for organizing story drafts, collecting research, and brainstorming ideas on the go.

   Why it matters: Writing pharmaceutical stories requires balancing science with emotion. These tools help refine your language while keeping it engaging.

   - **Visual Storytelling Tools**
     - Canva & Adobe Express— Perfect for creating infographics, patient journey visuals, and HCP explainer graphics.
     - Vynod & Doodly— Ideal for animated explainer videos to break down complex medical concepts engagingly.

- Lumen5 & Invideo— Convert blog content into short, engaging video stories for social media.

Why it matters: A strong visual element boosts recall and makes pharma storytelling more immersive, especially for audiences who prefer watching over reading.

- **Podcast & Audio Storytelling Tools**
  - Anchor & Descript— Great for creating and editing branded pharma podcasts featuring patient stories, doctor interviews, and treatment breakthroughs.
  - Otter.ai & Rev— Converts spoken narrative into text for repurposing into blogs, case studies, or whitepapers.

Why it matters: HCPs and patients consume more audio content today, whether through medical podcasts or patient advocacy interviews, so audio storytelling is necessary.

2. **Tools for Measuring Storytelling Impact**
   - **Social Media & Engagement Analytics**
     - Hootsuite & Sprout Social— Track engagement, shares, and comments to measure which pharma stories resonate most.
     - BuzzSumo— Analyzes top-performing content to see what is working in pharma storytelling worldwide.
     - BrandWatch— AI-powered sentiment analysis to understand how people feel about your brand stories.

   Why it matters: If a story is not engaging, it is not effective. Track and optimize based on real audience reactions.

   - **Website & Content Analysis**
     - Google Analytics— Tracks how users engage with your pharma content (time spent on page, bounce rate, click-throughs).

- Hotjar— Provides heatmaps and session recordings to see how people interact with your brand storytelling on your website.

Why it matters: A high bounce rate? Your story may not be engaging. A longer time on the page? Your storytelling is working. Refine accordingly!

- **ROI & Conversion Tracking**
  - HubSpot & Marketo— Tracks how storytelling impacts lead generation, HCP engagement, and patient education.
  - Tableau & Power BI— Analyze the impact of storytelling campaigns on brand performance and sales.

Why it matters: Storytelling is not just about inspiration—it should drive real business impact. These tools help prove your stories lead to action.

Final Thoughts: The Power of Data-Driven Storytelling

With these tools, you are not just telling stories—you are crafting strategic narratives that connect with the right people, in the right way, at the right time.

- Write smarter with AI-powered content tools.
- Enhance engagement with visual storytelling.
- Track impact with analytics and audience insights.

So, what story will you tell next? And more importantly, how will you measure its success?

Conclusion

20. The Timeless Power of Stories in Pharma Marketing
    - Summing Up: Key Insights
    - Embracing the Future of Storytelling

The Future of Pharma Marketing Belongs to Storytellers

At its core, pharmaceutical marketing has always been about more than just data and clinical claims—It's about human lives, struggles, and triumphs. And what better way to connect with people than through storytelling?

We have explored how stories build trust, educate, inspire action, and shape brand identity. Whether it is a patient overcoming a rare disease, a physician finding a breakthrough treatment, or a brand championing a cause, the most successful pharmaceutical companies are not just selling products but telling meaningful, purpose-driven stories.

But here is the exciting part—storytelling in pharma is still evolving.

- AI is personalizing narratives.
- Gamification is making stories interactive.
- Immersive technologies are creating unforgettable brand experiences.
- Data-driven insights are ensuing stories that drive real impact.

The future of pharmaceutical storytelling is dynamic, digital, and deeply human. As a brand marketer, you shape campaigns and how patients, HCPs, and stakeholders experience healthcare.

So, as you move forward, ask yourself:

What is the next great story your brand needs to tell? More importantly, how will you make it matter?

CHAPTER
20

The Timeless Power of Stories in Pharma Marketing

Think about the last time a story truly moved you. Maybe it was a patient's journey of resilience, a doctor's unwavering dedication, or a groundbreaking discovery that changed lives. These are not just narratives—they are powerful connections that stay with us.

In pharmaceutical marketing, stories are more than just tools; they bridge science and humanity. While data, clinical studies, and efficacy rates are essential, stories make these numbers meaningful.

Why? Because stories make people feel.

- A well-crafted patient story transforms an abstract medical condition into a real human experience.
- A physician's perspective brings credibility and trust, turning scientific advancements into actionable insights.
- A purpose-driven brand narrative resonates beyond features—it inspires belief and loyalty.

And here is the best part: While technologies evolve and trends shift, the core of storytelling remains unchanged. The pharmaceutical industry may be embracing AI, wearables, and immersive experiences. Still, at the heart of it all, the most successful brands will always be the ones that tell impactful stories.

When people remember a story, they don't just remember the facts but how it made them feel.

And that is the timeless power of storytelling in pharma marketing.

Summing Up Key Insights

We have traveled through the fascinating world of storytelling in pharmaceutical marketing, from its ancient roots to the cutting-edge technologies shaping its future. Along the way, we have uncovered why stories matter, how they build trust, and how they create meaningful connections with patients, healthcare professionals, and stakeholders.

Here are the key takeaways:

1. Stories are powerful because they make people feel. In a complex, data-driven industry, emotions create the human connection that facts alone cannot.
2. Trust is everything. In a highly regulated environment, authentic storytelling helps bridge the gap between scientific precision and patient-centered care.
3. Tailor stories for different audiences. What resonates with a patient might not work for a physician or an investor. Personalization is key.
4. Technology is revolutionizing storytelling. AI, VR, and digital platforms create immersive, interactive, and hyper-personalized narratives that engage audiences like never before.
5. The future of storytelling is data-driven and dynamic. AI can predict what messages will resonate, but storytelling must remain authentic, ethical, and human.

Final Thought

No matter how advanced pharmaceutical marketing becomes, one truth will always remain: People don't just buy products; they buy stories.

And brands that tell the most compelling, credible, and compassionate stories will be the ones that truly resonate.

Embracing the Future of Storytelling

The way we tell stories in pharmaceutical marketing is evolving faster than ever. New technologies, data-driven insights, and shifting audience expectations reshape how brands connect with patients, physicians, and stakeholders. But at its core, storytelling remains what it has always been—a powerful way to make people feel, think, and act.

So, how do we embrace this future?

- **Stay Human, Even in the Digital World**

  AI can personalize narratives and predict engagement, but authentic human experiences drive the most impactful stories. Patients, caregivers, and healthcare professionals connect with stories that reflect their realities, challenges, and hopes.

- **Leverage Emerging Technologies**

  Virtual reality (VR), augmented reality (AR), AI-generated content, and immersive digital platforms transform storytelling from passive consumption to interactive experiences. Imagine a patient entering a VR simulation to understand a disease journey or an AI-driven chatbot delivering real-time, personalized health education.

- **Create Stories that Adapt and Resonate**

  One-size-fits-all messaging is fading. The future belongs to fluid, multi-channel storytelling that adapts to the audience, whether through social media, wearable tech, or AI-powered engagement tools.

- **Balance Innovation with Ethics**

  As AI and data-driven storytelling grow, so do the ethical considerations. Transparency, accuracy, and trust should be at the heart of every pharma story. Responsible storytelling is not just good practice—it's essential for credibility.

Final Thought

The future of storytelling in pharma marketing is not just technology—it is about using technology to tell me more meaningful, impactful, and human-centric stories. The brands that embrace this evolution of authenticity, creativity, and integrity will be the ones that truly resonate.

Appendix

- Glossary of Key Terms in Storytelling
- Suggested Readings and References
- List of Tools and Platforms for Storytelling in Pharma Marketing
- Bibliography

Glossary of Key Terms in Storytelling

1. **Narrative Arc**: The Structure of a story, typically including a beginning (setup), middle (conflict), and end (resolution).
2. **Character**: The person or persona at the heart of a story, such as a patient, physician, or researcher, whose journey drives the narrative.
3. **Conflict**: The challenge or problem that creates tension in a story and keeps the audience engaged. In pharma, this could be a disease, a treatment challenge, or a healthcare barrier.
4. **Resolution** is the story's outcome. It often showcases a solution, breakthrough, or transformation, such as a patient's improved quality of life after treatment.
5. **Empathy**: The emotional connection a story creates, helping the audience relate to the characters and their experiences.
6. **Brand Narrative**: A strategic storytelling approach that defines how a brand communicates its mission, values, and impact through compelling stories.
7. **Emotional Appeal**: A technique that taps into human emotions (hope, fear, joy, trust) to make the message more memorable and impactful.
8. **Authenticity**: Ensure stories are real, credible, and relatable. This is especially crucial in pharma marketing, where trust is paramount.

9. **Patient-Centric Storytelling**: Placing the patient's experiences, struggles, and triumphs at the center of the narrative to create meaningful engagement.
10. **Metaphor & Analogy**: Using comparisons to simplify complex medical concepts (e.g., describing the immune system as a "body's defense army").
11. **Multi-Channel Storytelling**: Delivering a story across different platforms (social media, websites, videos, email campaigns) to maximize reach and impact.
12. **AI-Generated Storytelling**: Using artificial intelligence to personalize and generate narratives based on data and audience insights.
13. **Gamification**: Incorporating interactive and game-like elements in storytelling to enhance engagement, such as quizzes or virtual patient journeys.
14. **Augmented Reality (AR) & Virtual Reality (VR):** Technologies that immerse audiences in a story by creating interactive, 3D environments—helpful for explaining complex medical concepts.
15. **Data-Driven Storytelling**: Leveraging analytics and insights to craft stories tailored to specific audiences, ensuring relevance and effectiveness.
16. **Regulatory Compliance**: Ensuring storytelling aligns with industry guidelines (FDA, EMA, etc.), avoiding misleading claims or non-compliant messaging.
17. **Transparency**: Providing clear, accurate, evidence-based information to maintain credibility in pharma narratives.
18. **Privacy & Consent**: Adhering to patient privacy laws (e.g., GDPR, HIPAA) when sharing patient experiences or real-world evidence.

Suggested Readings and References

Books on Storytelling & Marketing

1. ***Made to Stick:*** *Why Some Ideas Survive and Others Die* – Chip Heath & Dan Heath: A must-read on why some messages resonate while others are forgotten. The Heath brothers break down the elements of compelling storytelling.
2. ***Building a Story Brand:*** *Clarify Your Message So Customers Will Listen* – Donald Miller: Explains how to use storytelling to build strong brand narratives that engage and persuade audiences.
3. **Jonathan Gottschall's *The Storytelling Animal:*** *How Stories Make Us Human* explores the psychology behind storytelling and why humans are wired for narratives.
4. ***Contagious*:** How to Build Word of Mouth in the Digital Age – Jonah Berger: Delves into why certain stories and messages go viral, with key lessons for marketers.
5. ***The Power of Moments:*** *Why Certain Experiences Have Extraordinary Impact* – Chip Heath & Dan Heath—Explains how brands can create memorable moments using storytelling to shape customer experiences.

Research & Articles on Pharma Storytelling

1. ***The Role of Storytelling in Healthcare and Pharma Marketing*** – Harvard Business Review. Explores how pharma companies are using narratives to build trust and engage patients and HCPs.
2. ***Narrative Medicine: Honoring the Stories of Illness, by*** **Rita** Charon, is a fascinating look at how storytelling is integrated into medicine to improve patient care.
3. ***Patient-Centered Pharma Marketing: The Power of Personal Stories*** – Journal of Medical Marketing. Discusses case studies of how pharma brands have successfully leveraged patient narratives.
4. ***AI and Storytelling: The Future of Personalized Marketing*** – MIT Technology Review

   Explains how artificial intelligence is transforming storytelling in the pharma and healthcare industries.

Online Resources & Blogs

- Content Marketing Institute (www.contentmarketinginstitute.com). A go-to resource for insights on storytelling in content marketing.
- Fierce Pharma Marketing (www.fiercepharma.com/marketing). Covers the latest trends and case studies in pharma marketing, including storytelling applications.
- Pharmaceutical Executive (www.pharmexec.com). Industry-specific insights on brand storytelling, patient engagement, and digital strategies.
  - TED Talks on Storytelling & Marketing
  - "The Secret Structure of Great Talks" – Nancy Duarte
  - "The Magical Science of Storytelling" – David JP Phillips

List of Tools and Platforms for Storytelling in Pharma Marketing

Storytelling in pharma marketing requires a blend of creativity, data, and technology. From content creation to distribution and measurement, the right tools can help marketers craft compelling narratives that resonate with patients, healthcare professionals (HCPs), and other stakeholders. Here's a categorized list of essential storytelling tools and platforms:

Content Creation & Storytelling Tools

1. Canva – User-friendly design tool for creating visuals, infographics, and social media posts to enhance storytelling.
2. Adobe Creative Cloud (Photoshop, Illustrator, Premiere Pro) – Professional suite for designing high-quality images, videos, and animations.
3. Visme – A great tool for creating engaging presentations, infographics, and data-driven visual stories.
4. InVideo – A video storytelling platform that enables marketers to create engaging brand stories with templates and AI-powered editing.
5. Synthesia – an AI-powered video creation tool that generates human-like avatars and voiceovers for personalized video storytelling.

6. Piktochart – For creating engaging infographics that simplify complex pharma data into digestible visuals.
7. Lumen5 – An AI-driven platform that converts blog posts and articles into engaging videos for multi-channel storytelling.

Storytelling & Content Writing Platforms

1. Grammarly & Hemingway Editor – For refining storytelling by improving readability, tone, and clarity of narratives.
2. Jasper AI – An AI-powered writing assistant that helps create compelling brand stories, patient narratives, and marketing content.
3. Scrivener – A long-form storytelling tool for structuring pharma brand narratives and patient journeys.
4. Notion & Evernote – For brainstorming and organizing storytelling ideas, research, and key messages.

Video & Interactive Storytelling Platforms

1. Powtoon – For creating animated explainer videos and educational content for pharma audiences.
2. Vyond – Helps create animated videos that make complex medical and scientific information engaging and digestible.
3. ThingLink – For adding interactive elements to images, videos, and infographics to create immersive brand experiences.
4. Shorthand – A no-code storytelling platform for building interactive, visually compelling narratives.
5. Racontr – For crafting interactive multimedia stories that blend text, images, video, and animations.

Social Media & Digital Storytelling Platforms

1. LinkedIn Stories & Articles – For sharing industry insights, patient success stories, and thought leadership in pharma marketing.

2. Instagram Reels & Stories – A powerful platform for sharing patient journeys, behind-the-scenes pharma stories, and product education.
3. Facebook & Twitter Threads – For bite-sized storytelling and brand engagement.
4. YouTube & TikTok – For video storytelling campaigns, influencer collaborations, and educational pharma content.
5. Medium – A platform for publishing long-form storytelling and thought leadership content in the pharma space.

Data-Driven Storytelling & Analytics

1. Google Data Studio – Transforms complex healthcare and pharma data into compelling visual stories.
2. Tableau – For interactive data storytelling using charts, dashboards, and real-world insights.
3. Power BI – A data visualization tool to create dynamic pharma stories backed by analytics.
4. Brandwatch – A Social listening tool that helps track the impact of brand storytelling across digital platforms.
5. Sprinklr – An AI-powered platform for measuring engagement and effectiveness of brand storytelling across multiple channels.
6. Hootsuite & Buffer – For scheduling, managing, and analyzing storytelling campaigns on social media.

Immersive & Emerging Technologies

1. Oculus VR & HTC Vive – For immersive virtual reality storytelling experiences in patient education and HCP engagement.
2. Unity & Unreal Engine – Game engines that power interactive storytelling, gamification, and AR/VR experiences in pharma.

3. Adobe Aero – For creating augmented reality (AR) storytelling experiences in marketing and education.
4. IBM Watson & OpenAI – For AI-driven content generation and predictive storytelling insights.

This toolkit empowers pharma marketers to craft compelling, data-driven, and immersive storytelling experiences that connect with multiple stakeholders. By integrating these tools into brand strategy, pharma companies can create narratives that inform, engage, and inspire action.

Bibliography

1. Heath, C., & Heath, D. (2007). Made to Stick: Why Some Ideas Survive and Others Die. Random House.
2. Guber, P. (2011). Tell to Win: Connect, Persuade, and Triumph with the Hidden Power of Story. Crown Business.
3. Simmons, A. (2006). The Story Factor: Inspiration, Influence, and Persuasion through the Art of Storytelling. Basic Books.
4. Fog, K., Budtz, C., & Yakaboylu, B. (2010). Storytelling: Branding in Practice. Springer.
5. Salmon, C. (2017). Storytelling: Bewitching the Modern Mind. Verso Books.
6. Godin, S. (2005). All Marketers Are Liars: The Power of Telling Authentic Stories in a Low-Trust World. Portfolio.
7. Duarte, N. (2010). Resonate: Present Visual Stories that Transform Audiences. Wiley.
8. Sachs, J. (2012). Winning the Story Wars: Why Those Who Tell (and Live) the Best Stories Will Rule the Future. Harvard Business Review Press.
9. Kotler, P., & Keller, K. L. (2016). Marketing Management. Pearson.
10. Trout, J., & Ries, A. (1981). Positioning: The Battle for Your Mind. McGraw-Hill.

11. Smith, M. (2019). Pharma Brand Management Strategies: Identifying and Overcoming Marketing Challenges in the Pharmaceutical Industry. Springer.
12. Kapferer, J. N. (2012). The New Strategic Brand Management. Kogan Page.
13. IMS Health. (2020). Global Pharma Marketing Trends Report.
14. Pharmaceutical Research and Manufacturers of America (PhRMA). (2021). Annual Industry Profile.
15. IQVIA. (2023). Digital Transformation in Pharma: Opportunities and Challenges.

Academic Research & Papers on Storytelling in Pharma

1. Brown, S., Kozinets, R. V., & Sherry, J. F. (2003). Teaching Old Brands New Tricks: Retro Branding and the Revival of Brand Meaning. Journal of Marketing, 67(3), 19–33.
2. Gilliam, D. A., & Flaherty, K. E. (2015). Storytelling by the Sales Force and Its Effect on Buyer-Seller Exchange. Industrial Marketing Management, 46, 132–142.
3. Gorry, G. A., & Westbrook, R. A. (2011). Once upon a Time: The Role of Rhetoric and Narrative in Management Research and Practice. Journal of Management Inquiry, 20(4), 406–411.
4. McKee, R., & Fryer, B. (2003). Storytelling That Moves People. Harvard Business Review, 81(6), 51–55.
5. Pine, B. J., & Gilmore, J. H. (1998). Welcome to the Experience Economy. Harvard Business Review, 76(4), 97–105.

Digital & AI-Driven Storytelling Resources

1. OpenAI. (2023). AI in Marketing: How Generative AI is Transforming Brand Storytelling.
2. McKinsey & Company. (2022). Personalization at Scale: The Next Big Leap in Pharma Marketing.
3. Forrester Research. (2021). How AI is Revolutionizing Pharma Storytelling and Brand Engagement.

4. Edelman Trust Barometer. (2023). Pharma & Healthcare: The Role of Trust in Effective Brand Communication.

Case Studies & Industry Examples

1. Pfizer. (2022). How Pfizer Used Storytelling to Build Trust During the Pandemic.
2. Novartis. (2021). The Power of Patient-Centric Storytelling: A Case Study.
3. Johnson & Johnson. (2020). Brand Storytelling in Healthcare: Lessons from J&J's "Campaign for Nursing's Future."
4. Roche. (2019). How Roche Uses Data-Driven Storytelling to Improve Patient Engagement.
5. GSK. (2021). The Role of Emotional Storytelling in Vaccine Awareness Campaigns.

About the Author

Subba Rao Chaganti

He has a master's in business administration and over fifty-two years of experience in

pharmaceutical marketing. His experience covers all facets of the industry, from selling to sales management, product management, and heading the total marketing activity. He has experience in domestic and international marketing and the Indian and multinational sectors.

He also taught a course on Advertising and Brand Management as an adjunct professor at Gitam Institute of Foreign Trade (now part of Gitam University) in Visakhapatnam for a few years and a course on Marketing as a visiting faculty member at Jawaharlal Nehru Technological University (JNTU) in Hyderabad.

He lives in Farmington, Connecticut, USA, and can be reached at: subbarao.chaganti@gmail.com.

Here is a list of his publications:

1. Pharmaceutical Marketing in India: Concepts, Cases, Strategy
2. Game Plans for Post-GATT Era: Action Agenda of Indian Pharmaceutical Industry

3. Compete or Forfeit: Strategies for Sustainable Competitive Advantage in Pharma Product Patents Era
4. Pharmaceutical Marketing in India for Today and Tomorrow - 25th Anniversary Edition
5. Bullseyes and Blunders: Lessons from 100 Cases in Pharma Marketing
6. Digital Pharma Marketing Playbook: Winning With the New Rules of Engagement
7. Cracking the Generics Code: Your Single-Source Success Manual for Winning in Multi-Source Product Markets
8. Reimagine Pharma Marketing: Make It Future-Proof!
9. Brand Positioning in Pharma
10. Transactional to Transformational Marketing in Pharma: The Science of Why and the Art of How!
11. A to Z of Pharmaceutical Marketing: World's First and Only Encyclopedia, set of 2 Volumes
12. The Synergy of Minds: Human+AI Orchestrating the Pharma Marketing Revolution
13. Design Thinking for Pharma: Forget Features, Focus on Feelings
14. The Pharma Product Manager: Handbook for Navigating the Digital Frontier
15. Sentiment Analysis for Pharma Marketers
16. Whispering to AI: Prompt Engineering for Pharma Brand Managers

www.ingramcontent.com/pod-product-compliance
Ingram Content Group UK Ltd.
Pitfield, Milton Keynes, MK11 3LW, UK
UKHW020218290926
15470UKWH00001B/267

9 789349 562035